BEYOND *the* HUSTLE

CONQUERING MENTAL HEALTH CHALLENGES IN ENTREPRENEURSHIP

MARK FUJIWARA

FOREWORD BY BLAKE MYCOSKIE, FOUNDER OF TOMS SHOES

ISBN: 978-1-964377-58-2 (ebook)

ISBN: 978-1-964377-57-5 (paperback)

ISBN: 978-1-964377-56-8 (hardcover)

The information provided in this book is for educational and informational purposes only. It is not intended as a substitute for professional medical advice, diagnosis or treatment. Always seek the advice of your physician or other qualified healthcare provider with any questions you may have regarding a medical condition or mental health concerns. The author and publisher of this book do not provide medical advice, nor do they assume any liability for the use of the information provided. Readers are encouraged to consult with appropriate professionals for specific advice tailored to their individual circumstances.

For more information about Mark Fujiwara,
scan the QR code below:

For my wife, Amy—a beautiful author in her own right—my partner in higher purpose and friend for life.

CONTENTS

FOREWORD

By Blake Mycoskie, founder of TOMS Shoes

I always had this gut sense I'd sell TOMS one day. What I never imagined was selling it for $400 million and feeling more lost than free.

It all started in 2006 on a dusty road in Argentina with a simple idea: give a pair of shoes for every pair sold. And somehow that turned into a global movement. TOMS became a for-profit business with a soul, and that soul gave me a reason to wake up every day. Even now, I still hold the title of Chief Shoe Giver. It's not just a nice line on a résumé. It's the proudest part of my life.

But when I sold the company in August 2014, something cracked open inside me. It was subtle at first—a tightness in my chest, a buzzing in my head I couldn't shut off. People congratulated me, and I smiled. But inside? I felt like I was sinking. And the money, all $400 million of it, didn't fix anything. If anything, it just made me feel more isolated. Like I'd run this incredible race and then someone turned off all the lights at the finish line.

The truth is, I had no clue who I was without TOMS.

I'd spent so many years tying my worth to impact, to hustle, to mission. And suddenly, I had no mission. No clarity. Just noise. I remembered something I wrote in *Start Something That Matters* back in 2011: "When you discover what your passion is, you will have found your story as well." I wanted to believe that still, but I couldn't hear my story anymore. I was numb.

And that's when things got dark.

I started chasing any hit of dopamine I could find. High risk hobbies. Parties. Shallow highs that left me emptier than I'd ever been. My marriage was falling apart and I was losing confidence as a parent. And every time I looked in the mirror, I saw someone who had everything—and somehow felt like nothing.

Then, a moment. A kid's birthday party of all places. I didn't want to be there. I was irritated and anxious and completely disconnected. And that's when I met Mark.

He asked me, "How are you *really* doing?" And something about how he said it made me drop the mask. Ninety seconds into meeting, we were talking about suicidal thoughts, depression and everything I was too ashamed to admit to anyone else. It was like meeting someone who spoke my language, a language most people are too afraid to learn— entrepreneurial despair.

Mark didn't give me advice. He gave me space. Space to say, "I'm not okay" without fearing judgment. And slowly, through long hikes, unfiltered conversations and his deep presence, I started to peel back the layers. I talked about my faulty bipolar diagnosis, about the meds that made me feel like a ghost in my own body. I admitted how lonely it is to be seen as "the successful one" when inside you feel like you're crumbling.

I tried everything. Western medicine. Therapy. And eventually alternative healing—ayahuasca, microdosing, plant medicine. They didn't *fix* me, but they helped me remember who I was underneath all the noise. They helped me detox from more than substances. I detoxed from validation, from perfectionism, from the need to always be the guy with the answers.

And in the quiet, I found my story again.

These days, I tell that story on a podcast called No Magic Pill. I speak out loud the things most founders feel but are too afraid to say: that success without inner peace is just another kind of poverty, that you can build something world-changing and still feel broken inside. After the big exit, the hardest work isn't finding your next company—it's finding your way back to yourself.

Mark helped me do that. He helped me see that entrepreneurship and mental health aren't separate conversations. They're the same one. And that's what this book is about.

If you're reading this and you've ever felt like the world celebrates your highlight reel while you suffer behind the scenes... this book is for you.

If you've ever had millions in your account and still lain in bed wondering what the hell the point of any of it is...this book is for you.

And if you've ever needed someone to say, "You're not crazy, and you're not alone," this book is for you too.

We need more honesty in our entrepreneurial culture. More grace. More spaces to break down without breaking apart.

I'm still learning. Still healing. But I'm here. And I'm grateful.

Here's to telling the truth, even when it's messy.

With love,

Blake

INTRODUCTION

One must still have chaos in oneself to be able to give birth to a dancing star.
—Friedrich Nietzsche

Brilliant entrepreneurs often walk the same path. Their personality traits—creativity, perfectionism, risk-taking, hyper-focus, determination—make them perfectly suited for success, but they can also impact mental health. And those bright shining stars turn supernova or, like a shooting star, jettison themselves headlong into oblivion as their legacy flashes across the night sky.

Because of the stigma around mental health in our society, alternatives to the shooting-star ending have been rare. We have yet to embrace the pervasiveness of mental health issues, all of which transcend socioeconomic strata, race, color and creed. My upbringing by Chinese and Japanese parents informed my own complicated relationship to mental health and what is considered acceptable. But stigma—and my long-conflicted mindset—are starting to change amidst the global mental health crisis we find ourselves in.

New treatment modalities and the openness with which

we've begun to address mental health as a society are changing the face of how we view and approach treatment. Talking about mental health isn't so taboo anymore. Treatment modalities have begun to embrace the whole human. While we still have a way to go, the simple transparency of recognizing mental health as an essential component of well-being has the power to create a sea change as impactful as a cure for cancer—and the tragic, shooting-star ending can transform to one of inspiration and metamorphosis.

With three decades in the private wealth management industry, I've been privy to so many stars losing their light.

I myself grappled with a near-missed opportunity to shine beyond my achievements. A large percentage of my clients are entrepreneurs and my purpose in serving them has always extended beyond their finances—I'm interested in making sure they'll be around to enjoy their wealth. And that has increasingly come to mean caring about their mental health as well. Developing close relationships with clients and colleagues over the years, I've come to realize just how many entrepreneurs struggle with their mental health—these pioneers who work, live and think outside the box. I recognize their struggles as my own.

For many, the road from startup to exit is paved with sacrifices, sleepless nights and relentless determination.

The toll on mental well-being often goes unnoticed. In the bustling landscape of entrepreneurship, the spotlight falls on success stories—the triumphs, breakthroughs and innovations that fuel the spirit of enterprise. Behind those glittering narratives lies a far dimmer reality—these daring forerunners and boundary breakers face silent struggles, inner battles and mental health challenges. High-functioning achievers find themselves isolated, lonely and at a loss for how to spend their time without productivity and earning as their primary deliverables.

This book is a clarion call: let this be the day, from this point forward, that we can safely and openly speak about our mental health—as plainly as we speak about the common cold. Because it's that pervasive. Yet it remains a taboo subject, a hidden illness —perhaps for the very fact that it is hidden. But our age of science is producing new attitudes and new treatment modalities for mental health—like Transcranial Magnetic Stimulation, effective in treating depression when medication doesn't help and the Science of Psychedelics, where neuroscience meets psychology— that are changing the face of treatment and the conversation around mental health.

I am honored and humbled to share my framework for living and working within the Japanese concepts of *ikigai, ichigo ichie* and *kintsugi*. I will also speak about author Jim Collins's "Plus Two" approach to valuing our finite time on this planet. By measuring our own frequencies, as well as those we spend the most time with, we discover how to preserve precious time and energy to devote to our higher purpose.

We learn to ask ourselves three of the most simple yet transformative questions possible:

1. What are you doing?
2. Who are you doing it with?
3. What is your energy like?

Throughout these interviews, you will read about what it means to create emotional, spiritual and financial capital doing what you love with the gifts you have—*ikigai*—in the pursuit of finding a higher purpose. We will speak about what it is to value our time in the present moment—*ichigo ichie*, "one opportunity, one encounter"—with respect to those we are intentional about spending our time with. And finally, these conversations offer perspectives that shift with an evolving mindset—*kintsugi*— healing our mental health and addiction issues by gilding them with the attitude that all things are in service to our higher purpose.

Through interviews with some of the most innovative minds of our time—both entrepreneurs and mental health practitioners breaking boundaries in their fields—we'll talk about how mental health is impacted from startup to exit.

We'll explore treatment modalities that are also outside the box and actionable ways to create healthier mental well-being without the use of pharmaceuticals. Finally, we'll focus on the importance of inclusion and community. You see, my passion for destigmatizing mental wellness is personal. Most of my life—though it took me a long time to admit it—I struggled with mental health issues. Not being able to talk about it almost ended my life. But when I finally found the ability to speak about my struggles, to find others who shared in my experience, it was literally a lifesaver.

A key theme that develops among entrepreneurs is the decline of mental health after they've exited the companies they founded, or even during the process itself. This book is a testament to the journey that begins where the entrepreneurial narrative often ends—after the exit, when the adrenaline of the startup saga subsides and the realities of life beyond the business take center stage. It is at this point that the exit reflects a kind of entrapment where it doesn't feel safe to leave, not completely. The void an exit creates can easily become an entryway to myriad circles of hell, marked by profound transitions, unforeseen obstacles and the enduring quest for purpose and meaning in the aftermath of success. And yet, there is always a light: for many, their dark nights have led to a journey of the soul, a metamorphosis of the true self toward a higher calling.

So there it is: out in the open. In the pages that follow, read, listen, digest. Discover the new frontiers of mental health treatment and why they work when traditional treatments fail. And don't be afraid to share your own experiences.

NON-TRADITIONAL MODALITIES—THE FUTURE OF MENTAL HEALTH

There's an exciting new frontier in healthcare: nontraditional modalities for treating mental health. Before we turn to our interviews, we'll explore some of the innovative new treatments that will be discussed by the mental health practitioners—providing a framework for the state of mental healthcare today and shining a light on the reasons traditional methods have failed so many for so long. As inclusion and community continue to build around the topic of mental wellness, these innovative treatment options—pioneered by physicians who are entrepreneurial in their own right, breaking new ground by envisioning novel approaches to age-old problems—hold the potential to transform the landscape of mental wellness.

Transcranial Magnetic Stimulation (TMS)

A non-invasive procedure that uses magnetic pulses to stimulate specific regions of the brain involved in mood regulation and implicated in mental health disorders, TMS has proven effective in treating depression. In particularly difficult or treatment-resistant cases, TMS can be hugely beneficial, underscoring its potential to revolutionize psychiatric care by offering an alternative to medication and therapy.

With repeated sessions of TMS, the brain's neural circuits may undergo changes in connectivity and activity patterns—a process known as neuroplasticity, which is believed to play a crucial role in the therapeutic effects of TMS. Over time, these changes can lead to improvements in mood and the symptoms of depression. TMS has also shown promise in the treatment of other conditions, such as anxiety disorders, bipolar disorder and certain types of schizophrenia.

A significant advancement in the field of mental health treatment, TMS offers a safe, effective and well-tolerated option for people who may be hesitant to pursue traditional psychiatric treatments due to stigma or fear of side effects. This modality—

with its non-pharmacological, non-invasive nature—can serve as a more palatable option. As research continues and technology advances, TMS may become an even more integral part of mental healthcare, serving as a beacon of hope for individuals grappling with treatment-resistant mental health conditions.

NON-TRADITIONAL MODALITIES
THE FUTURE OF MENTAL HEALTH

THERE'S AN EXCITING NEW FRONTIER IN HEALTHCARE: nontraditional modalities for treating mental health. Before we turn to our interviews, we'll explore some of the innovative new treatments that will be discussed by the mental health practitioners—providing a framework for the state of mental healthcare today and shining a light on the reasons traditional methods have failed so many for so long. As inclusion and community continue to build around the topic of mental wellness, these innovative treatment options—pioneered by physicians who are entrepreneurial in their own right, breaking new ground by envisioning novel approaches to age-old problems—hold the potential to transform the landscape of mental wellness.

TRANSCRANIAL MAGNETIC STIMULATION (TMS)

A non-invasive procedure that uses magnetic pulses to stimulate specific regions of the brain involved in mood regulation and implicated in mental health disorders, TMS has proven effective in treating depression. In particularly difficult or treatment-resistant cases, TMS can be hugely beneficial, underscoring its potential to revolutionize psychiatric care by offering an alternative to medication and therapy.

With repeated sessions of TMS, the brain's neural circuits may undergo changes in connectivity and activity patterns—a process known as neuroplasticity, which is believed to play a crucial role in the therapeutic effects of TMS. Over time, these changes can lead to improvements in mood and the symptoms of depression. TMS has also shown promise in the treatment of other conditions, such as anxiety disorders, bipolar disorder and certain types of schizophrenia.

A significant advancement in the field of mental health treatment, TMS offers a safe, effective and well-tolerated option for people who may be hesitant to pursue traditional psychiatric treatments due to stigma or fear of side effects. This modality—with its non-pharmacological, non-invasive nature—can serve as a more palatable option. As research continues and technology advances, TMS may become an even more integral part of mental healthcare, serving as a beacon of hope for individuals grappling with treatment-resistant mental health conditions.

PSYCHEDELIC-ASSISTED THERAPY

Psychedelic therapy offers a novel and potentially transformative approach to treating mental illness, particularly in cases where other modalities have failed. Psychedelics like psilocybin (found in certain mushrooms) and MDMA (commonly known as ecstasy) are used in conjunction with psychotherapy to treat conditions like depression, PTSD, anxiety addiction and existential distress in patients with life-threatening illnesses.

Psychedelic therapy sessions are conducted under the guidance of trained therapists in a safe environment. The therapist provides psychological support and facilitates the therapeutic process while the individual experiences the effects of the psychedelic substance—which prompt profound alterations in perception, cognition and consciousness. These altered states of consciousness often lead to heightened introspection, emotional openness and emotional processing and may enable individuals to access deeply buried emotions, memories and insights that are difficult to reach through conventional therapy alone. Clinical trials have reported significant and enduring reductions in symptoms, improvements in mood and enhanced quality of life following psychedelic-assisted therapy.

A paradigm shift in mental health treatment, psychedelic therapy offers a holistic approach that transcends diagnostic categories, going beyond symptom management to address root causes—the underlying psychological, emotional and existential issues that contribute to mental suffering. Recognizing the interconnectedness of mind, body and spirit, psychedelic therapy promotes healing at multiple levels of an individual's being and can result in personal transformation.

FUNCTIONAL MENTAL HEALTH

Myriad other holistic modalities fall under the umbrella of Functional Mental Health: mindfulness and meditation, nutritional psychiatry, art and music therapy, nervous system regulation and lifestyle. Functional mental health—which refers to a person's ability to cope with the daily demands of life, maintain healthy relationships and contribute effectively to society— focuses on the capacity to engage in activities of daily living, pursue meaningful goals and experience overall well-being, even in the presence of mental health symptoms or diagnoses.

Functional Mental Health emphasizes the holistic well-being of individuals, recognizing that mental health is not just the absence of illness, but also the presence of strengths, resilience and the ability to lead fulfilling lives. It encompasses a broad spectrum of factors that contribute to overall capability and quality of life, regardless of mental health diagnoses or symptoms. Key aspects of Functional Mental Health include adaptive coping skills, social and interpersonal relationships, occupational and educational engagement, self-identity and purpose and resilience and recovery—strategies for mastering daily living that can be used in concert with other treatment modalities— whether traditional or nontraditional.

These new approaches to treatment reveal a shift in the way mental health is perceived in society, sweeping mental illness out from under the rug and acknowledging that mental health is a common ailment—much like the common cold. Ascribing value to the whole human in the approach to treatment is not only expanding the toolkit of mental health practitioners but also challenging conventional paradigms and stigmas surrounding mental illness. By embracing diverse approaches that honor the complexity of human experience, we can foster a more inclusive, multidimensional approach to mental healthcare that prioritizes individual needs, preferences and strengths. We still have a long way to go. But as research and innovation continue to propel the field forward, the horizon of mental illness holds the promise of greater understanding, resilience and hope for all.

INCLUSION & COMMUNITY
WHAT WE ALL CAN DO

As we acknowledge that we still have a long way to go in changing the perception of mental health and the reception of mental illness in our society, we must beg the question: **What can I do?**

Lasting change begins with each of us. And what's becoming clear in these new approaches to treatment is that mental health affects us all. Each of us shares in this very human malady—and keeping our struggles secret is not the answer. Whether it's a strong case of the blues, grief over losing a loved one or the stress and anxiety visited upon us daily in our world of technology, transparency is the answer. Shame has no place in the treatment of any illness—it serves only to exacerbate the pain, further exposing an open wound. Embracing our humanity is the answer. So how can we do this?

Not feeling free to discuss my own struggles nearly ended me.

When my cousin committed suicide in his early 20s, it rocked my family. The loss of such a young life—especially through the act of self-destruction—was devastating. But it hit me hardest. We'd been so close. And I remembered the look I'd seen on his face recently...it was familiar; I'd felt those feelings myself. He was lost inside, the same as me. But in our family, you didn't talk about your feelings, your mistakes, your struggles. Would he still be alive today if he could have...if he had support? We'll never know.

So I couldn't even admit to myself that I was struggling. I went to college, got married, had kids...and then the world came crashing down on me. I still hadn't gotten help with my mental health struggles and now they were devouring me. I continued to bury my feelings, deny the moment, until finally I became suicidal. I had a plan for how I would end my life—all that was left to consider was the follow-through.

And that's when I called my cousin, the earth mother of my generation, who revealed her own issues with mental health. This turned my world around and opened the floodgates to a new life. I was able to talk about this with another human being; I unearthed a truth that wasn't just my truth—it was my family's truth and the truth of so many people I already knew and would encounter in my business life who suffer from mental health struggles and mental illness.

Inclusion and community saved my life. They are essential components of mental wellness and providing and receiving support fosters a sense of belonging and connection, crucial elements of well-being. So...what can you do?

Seek and Offer Social Support: Being part of a community provides encouragement, understanding and practical assistance in challenging times, helping us cope with stress and adversity and fostering resilience, coping skills and adaptive responses to life's ups and downs, enhancing our overall well-being. Inclusion and community involvement also combat social isolation—a significant risk factor for mental health struggles. Loneliness and isolation increase the rates of depression, anxiety, substance abuse and other mental health disorders.

Foster Validation and Affirmation, a Sense of Belonging: Feeling accepted, valued and included contributes to a positive sense of self-esteem and identity, a fundamental element of human well-being and essential for maintaining our mental health. Inclusive communities provide solace—a space where we can express ourselves authentically and feel valued and appreciated by others and experience feelings of fulfillment, meaning and security. The simple realization that we are not alone in what can feel like a harsh psychological landscape ameliorates our sense of anxiety and foreboding and fosters a sense of belonging. When we feel like we belong, we're far more likely to have a greater sense of purpose and meaning in our lives.

Embrace Diverse Perspectives | Empowerment and Advocacy: The empathy, understanding and tolerance engendered by inclusive communities promotes interconnectedness and exposes us to diverse perspectives that challenge the stigma, stereotypes and discrimination related to mental health issues. Diverse communities empower us to advocate for ourselves and others—creating a more supportive and inclusive environment for everyone. Through collective action, communities can work together to promote mental health awareness, education and access to resources—and eventually result in a society where we can talk about our mental health as easily as we discuss our physical ailments.

INTERVIEWS

IN THE INTERVIEWS THAT FOLLOW, I'LL BE SHARING THE ENCOUNTERS of entrepreneurs who've exited their startups and struggled with their mental health along the way, often encountering the biggest hurdles after the exit—when the pressures that once fueled the drive to succeed morph into a different kind of burden—one marked by uncertainty, identity crisis and the struggle to find fulfillment. The exit—far from providing the solace and predictability they expected—turns into a rollercoaster ride of emotions for these entrepreneurs who poured their hearts and souls into building their companies.

In story after story, we'll see that the transition out of the startup triggers a profound self-reckoning, leading to an identity crisis as they navigate life post-exit. And as they step away from the day-to-day operations, they grapple with feelings of loss, uncertainty, even failure—regardless of the exit outcome. The end of a startup can trigger an identity crisis as entrepreneurs redefine themselves beyond their roles as founders or CEOs, as they struggle to answer the question, "Who am I now?" Without the structure and mission of their startup framing their identity, they may feel adrift, disconnected, cowed by external pressures to replicate past success or transition into a new venture. Forced to confront questions about their identity, purpose and values, these individuals come to realize that their startups were so intertwined with their sense of self, they now face the challenge of separating their personal identity from their professional success. And looking back upon that success story, they often don't like what they see.

Another theme that develops is one of metamorphosis, as the universe intervenes once more and despite the challenges, the narrowing exit presents an opportunity for transformation and personal growth. Having had the opportunity to explore new interests, passions and roles outside the startup ecosystem, some entrepreneurs choose to pursue philanthropy, mentorship or investment, leveraging their experiences to make a positive impact in the world in a variety of ways. Others take a break to recharge, travel or spend time with loved ones while embarking on a new venture or discovering their life's purpose. In the end, these prodigies—who burst out of the startup gates, fought the battles of the business landscape then struggled through the harsh realities of reexamining and rebuilding a life after the exit —come to realize that everything they thought they wanted and fought for so ruthlessly, doesn't reflect their true self in the slightest. The millions of dollars they thought would set their minds at ease don't carry an ounce of weight in the stark reality of self-reckoning. They discover underlying meaning in their new role as an exited entrepreneur, living intentionally, measuring the value of their time in a drastically different way. Through introspection after the exit, a new self emerges—one that gleans at long last a higher state of being, a true purpose— and a transformation occurs that results in the perfect alignment of their higher purpose to the benefit of humanity.

The stories of these entrepreneurs will be interspersed with interviews with mental health practitioners who foster treatment modalities beyond prescription medication. Since the substance of the entrepreneur interviews will include treatment, we can dovetail specific stories or issues with insights from practitioners and delve into various modalities—so that we're not simply bringing the conversation around mental health to the table but also educating, offering light and hope: both from the success stories of recovery and available treatments.

IAN LOPATIN

Ian Lopatin is the founder of Spiritual Gangster, the co-founder of The Cools and Pry Financials and has exited three multimillion-dollar businesses.

Ian Lopatin is an entrepreneur best known for founding Spiritual Gangster, alongside his wife, Vanessa, by creating a lifestyle brand that blends spirituality with style.

I consider meeting Ian to be one of the most fortuitous connections I've ever made. We share the same values and I am humbled to know that someone with as much vision as Ian has continued to share his gifts with the world. He is one of the most prominent exited entrepreneurs I know, and one of the most determined people on the planet.

MARK FUJIWARA [MF]: Really good to be talking with you today. For those reading, would you mind sharing the story of how we first met?

IAN LOPATIN (IL): Happy to. So we first met initially through a mutual friend who's in my mastermind group. At first, when you and I got to talking, it was mostly financial, but over time, we became more friendly. You were speaking to a friend of mine, Joe Polish, at his mastermind down there. Then you invited me to speak to *your* mastermind. I did that, and then we just got more and more connected.

MF: So I wanted to get a sense from you as an entrepreneur, what your experience has been like exiting Spiritual Gangster, and how that has affected you.

IL: The first business I exited was a company called At One Yoga. I was an entertainment lawyer in Los Angeles for my job, and in 1999 I opened up At One Yoga in Arizona, which we sold in 2013 to Lifetime Fitness. That was my first big exit. Spiritual Gangster was the house brand for our yoga studio originally— my wife was making all these designs, my kids were tagging them and we were shipping them out of our house. Spiritual Gangster was an expensive hobby that turned into a business when we sold the yoga company in 2013. Before the boom and scale of the yoga business, I was kind of getting exhausted. I was teaching yoga every day 365 days a year, and we were open from seven in the morning to nine at night. I just wanted to find something that we could use to take a lot of the touch points and the learning that we got from yoga around mindfulness and a healthier lifestyle, things like teachings from Wayne Dyer and Eckhart Tolle and Deepak, and figure out a way to take that message to a bigger audience.

Spiritual Gangster was really born from the yoga studios, but we realized that it had a much more global appeal, where the yoga studios made sense because we built this incredible local brand and we also were the teacher training engine for all of Lifetime Fitness. We had an amazing yoga business, but it was also like a restaurant in the way it was harder to scale. So we were trying to find something where we could take the same ethos and build a broader community and apply it to retail production as opposed to a localized business service.

MF: What was your experience like when the business became scalable? How were you able to remove yourself from the daily operations?

IL: It was a super long journey, and we were really hands-on for a while. My wife was our Creative Director. For a while, I was the CEO then I stepped into the Chairman role. And it was just a long journey. It was traveling a lot of winding roads. I mean, we were very day-to-day, everyday. For the first 10 years, we hired a great CEO who did really well but ended up leaving right before COVID. And then we hired a president who was day-to-day and was a decent operator, but he completely took the brand off track. The brand lost some of its caché. He moved a lot of the products being made to China.

Over that same time, we added some people to our board, and my wife and I almost got pushed out of our own business, which was really, really challenging. So that was a very hard thing, because we built this business that we loved so much, and then we brought in some other investors and people who weren't really of the same mindset aligned with us. We went from loving our business to literally fighting every day to not get pushed out of it, then sort of watching it move away from a straight upward trajectory to flat, then into decline. Every year we grew five million bucks a year for like six years, and then it had two years where it went in the other direction.

We ended up firing that CEO and turning over the entire staff, and then we had to recap the business. We still own a piece of it today, but we got diluted and really got out of the day-to-day. The brand is back and moving well, but it was sort of bitter-sweet for us. There were a lot of challenges along the way bringing in people with whom we didn't resonate—and then people who we let into our business who really just tried to push us out of our own business, moving it in the wrong direction. That was really hard, to be honest.

The customer maybe didn't see the differences in the imme-diate term, but they would have seen the quality go down at some point. The vibe of the business got off track, and that's what was so important to us, because we built it on these high ideals, around building community and attracting the right people. We got on the cap table, and we let in some of the wrong people. The business was heading in a really bad direction where it kind of lost its way and lost its vibe, now it's moving back in the right direction. We have a CEO who I'm friends with, but economically, we didn't have the outcome that we thought we were going to have. We had the business sold to Bain, which was going to be an enormous financial win. But all of that ended up happening a lot differently than we expected.

MF: I'm sure there were difficulties in how that affected your entire family and the dynamics with you all successfully working together. Taking an abrupt turn like that would be extremely tough.

How do you spend your time these days?

IL: I wake up and I meditate every morning. I start my day at

5:30 am and I meditate. And I'm in recovery now. I go to morning meetings from 7:00 am to 8:00 am. Now I'm doing *The Artist's Way*. I do these morning pages every morning based on that book. I'll do a journaling session too. So that's kind of how I start my day. I feel like how you start your day is really how your day goes—and ultimately how your life goes. I am very, very intentional with how my days begin.

MF: Do you think recovery has given you a different perspective on your business and how you want things to look in the future?

IL: For sure. I'm just so much more clear. I'm actually really grateful, because I was suffering a lot as we sort of lost control of the business, and had to recap it. I recently spent six weeks in India. When I came back I started going to AA, and I think it's affected everything in my life. I'm definitely way more present now. But I think that if I had the financial outcome I was expecting with the business—or had I not gone through all the suffering with the business—I wouldn't have gone to India for that length of time. I don't think I would have gotten sober either.

Spiritual Gangster taught me amazing lessons. The suffering and the struggles around it, and when things were really challenging with addictions. It's worth it because you want to check out if you're not present there. And I was in so much stress around this business that I love so much, but I feel like now I'm in such a better place. I'm so much clearer and I have so much more energy and clarity.

And I'm really grateful for my journey and that I have an incredible sponsor. I've met a ton of people through AA, and it's another wonderful community. I was there the other morning listening to people share at a meeting, and I thought, *If the entire world were honest like people in AA, we'd be living on an amazing planet*. But I think, like a lot of things with addiction, it's hard to be honest with yourself. You sort of want to check out from your problems, unlike how things are now; I'm super grateful for my journey, all of it. I also think it was the mix of spending six weeks in India and going really deep with my teachers. I'm not suffering over anything anymore.

Our oldest daughter just got diagnosed for the second time with cancer, but I've been able to handle it so much better this time by being present for her and my wife and just being there without suffering. To just be really present. It's a tremendous tool that's helped me a ton, and I'm super grateful for it. I think if I had not had the struggles around the business, I wouldn't be sober right now.

MF: I'm really sorry to hear your daughter's going through that, but at the same time, I'm glad that you have that perspective and presence for her. It probably makes things feel lighter and maybe less scary for her.

IL: It's all about being present. The mind always wants to project this future that's gonna be terrible. You're gonna be broke, or you're gonna die or get sick. But that's not really the case. So it's about just being with things as they are, and having a really good vision for the future that things are going to work out. Before I got into recovery—and before I went to India—I realized I was suffering a lot. But I didn't see that it was because of my own thought process, and I've since learned my obsessive self was the source of all my suffering.

From there, I just got a lot clearer. It's about being awake, alert and clear. And then also, our business was always built to be of service. I told people, "It's a movement in the guise of a clothing company." Now combined with AA, it's helping other people be of service. I'm just way more intentional about those things. Now it's gotten way better. It's been a really awesome journey, not one that I thought I would take last year. I'm super grateful to be here after coming back from India before I got sober, when my drug use had just escalated so much. It went from one night this to one night that and then eventually everything all at once. I just knew I needed to change course.

MF: What prompted you to go to India? Do you think that was an intuitive thing for you?

IL: I know teachers [who] have all been trying to get me to go to India. I was firm: *I'm absolutely not going to India. I am not interested.* But I had two friends of mine who are doctors, who went and did this course. One of them is a radiologist who had 4000 radiologists working under his direction, but he was suicidal. He was super unhappy, suffering and struggling, just as I was going through this stuff with our business a year ago in November. I met him and his wife for lunch, and he looked incredible. I mean, he was like, 25 pounds lighter, but it was really that he had this glow about him.

He said, "Well, I went to India and it literally changed my entire life." So I left that lunch, and I immediately told my wife I had to go to India, and I was gonna go for two weeks.

Then I was there for my birthday in January, and after 10 days, I called my wife and said, "I know what I want for my birthday: I need to stay here and finish this program." And I did just that. Then I kind of took some time off, and the fear pendulum swung the whole other way. I got sober, went to AA and went back to India and spent another two weeks in the program. It was life-changing. I just sent Blake there.

MF: There seem to be patterns with all sorts of entrepreneurs I've noticed, especially in overcoming addiction and finding purpose. It sounds like you have a lot more living to do, and possibly more business ventures. It seems like there's a lot of hopefulness in your story.

IL: Yeah, I feel like I'm in a great place. I just finished a book I've been working on for four years. I'm launching that in the next month or two. That's been really great. I've started to do some speaking again and teaching more. I feel like I'm creating the next version of myself. I've got a lot of hard-earned wisdom that I'm excited to share.

MF: Are you still teaching yoga?

IL: I'm not teaching yoga, but I do teach enlightenment and

meditation. There's some yoga in it–less Asana–but it's primarily a lot of breathing and meditation and talking. But I still do teach yoga on occasion, for sure.

MF: Have you ever traveled specifically to teach yoga or meditation?

IL: I've taught all over the world. I used to be a headliner at all these yoga conferences, and I taught at Bonnaroo with a couple thousand people in the audience in the morning before the festivals. I taught at Rothbury with Michael Fronti. We had like 5000 people on the field, and he was doing the music while I was teaching yoga. But I've also taken groups all over Mexico and taught in New York, Italy, Peru. Now I'm doing a little bit more speaking. So it's less physical Asana. It's more, you know, like this week, I just taught it to 6000 Jewish kids from 60 countries, and I talked about enlightenment and meditation at the biggest congregation and gathering of Jewish youth outside of Israel. So it's cool I'm getting to talk to YPO [Young Presidents' Organization] and business leaders, but I'm also getting to talk to kids, which is phenomenal.

MF: Do you see yourself either integrating meditation or having that be more of a focus for you moving forward in your professional life?

IL: Oh, for sure. I have not missed many meditations in six months. I do it every single day. I do that more consistently than brushing my teeth. We have a YPO form retreat right now. We're meditating with our group, and I definitely feel like meditation is the base of everything that I do going forward. I've been doing some form of it for 20 years, but the technology that I've got from my teachers in India—at Ekam [a mystic meditation space, referring to the highest state of non-dual consciousness that can experience oneness while in the human body]—and its oneness is just the most incredible meditation technology, and they're very user-friendly, and they're super profound. I'm a huge believer in meditation, and it's a huge part of my life, so I don't ever miss doing it. It's a non-negotiable for me, sort of like not drinking. I meditate every day and I don't drink. Those are two of the main things that are part of who I am now.

MF: It seems like there is a modern resurgence with meditation. It's part of this movement that's caught on—kind of a spiritual practice, including cold plunges. Maybe things that have in the past seemed like alternatives or holistic healing-type things are becoming more mainstream.

IL: I've been cold plunging for eight or nine years consistently. I'm a huge believer. I also do the infrared sauna every day. I do the cold plunge, and I move and stretch. I think those are all part of what mental health is about. It's like your mind is the source of all your suffering. You know, my Indian guru says there are only two states. There's a suffering state and there's a non-suffering state. There is no third state. I was suffering for a long time. And so is almost everyone I know—with addiction problems or mental health problems. Medication is a very important tool to be able to manage your own life. And I think a lot of these things were maybe sort of on the fringe—the way yoga was on the fringe when I started our yoga studios 25 years ago—but now they are very mainstream. And I feel like meditation and all this stuff have real health benefits. It's about bringing yourself to the present.

MF: Yeah, that's amazing. Do you have anything you want to add? Any words of wisdom?

IL: I think the hardest person to get honest with is yourself. Recovery is about that. You stop trying to be someone else or hiding or trying to hide behaviors. It's just been a huge relief for me. I always say that one of the things I got from AA, words of wisdom, is that the opposite of addiction is connection. That really is the formula for happiness. If you connect with others and your focus is outside of yourself, your life gets a lot better.

My mom always used to say, "There's a reason why illness starts with "I" and wellness starts with "we." You've got to put the oxygen mask on yourself first, but then it's really about helping others, right? That's what we're here to do. I think that you're doing this with your work and with this book; you're helping entrepreneurs create community.

And that's really important—whether you're an entrepreneur or not. I have the luxury of being part of YPO, which is a very good peer group. But a lot of these people are lonely. It's the same thing with addicts. You don't think anyone can relate to you and that you're going through all these struggles by your-self. You're in your own mind. Once you start to connect with a community and help others, your life starts to change.

Another piece of wisdom: I always set the bar really high for myself. For example, I'm a golfer. If I didn't shoot even par, I thought I sucked at golf. If I wasn't at the top of my class in law school, I thought I was failing. What I realized in India was that I was setting the bar so high for enlightenment. Like, "Oh, when I get enlightened, I'm going to have all these magical powers." But the whole idea is that you gotta set the bar low so you can win. There's just really no reason to set the bar so high and make your life miserable. I think that's part of one of the greatest things I could understand. You don't need this $100 million exit. It's really about having these little wins on a daily basis and cele-brating your wins, but also rigging the game in your favor. You don't necessarily need to be the best, and actually, when you become the best, your life isn't even that much better. It's the journey—enjoy it—not the destination.

What I've realized about my journey of enlightenment is that no one's enlightened all the time. That's why every morning, I start off with those practices I spoke about in the beginning. The default state is one where your mind is worrying and it's fearful, but if you can change your default state through doing a lot of things—we talked about meditation and cold plunging—that's what it's all about. Your state will change throughout the day. So you have to find these practices. And the person to bring you back into that non-suffering is you, it's a beautiful thing.

I spend a lot of time with Tony Robbins, and he talks about people going, "Okay, you have to achieve this. Achieve this, achieve that. And before you achieve this, go, set your sights on what you're going to achieve next. And then we're gonna go do that." Ultimately, the issue is that you can't achieve your way to happiness, because one of three things happens: either you set your mind on something and you never get it, you're unhappy or you do get it and all you want is more of it. Or you get it only to find out that you wanted something else altogether.

I have a lot of friends who are very successful in business, and they'll say, "I want to make $10 million and then I want to make $100 million." So it's like, you're never enough, all of it is never enough. Or the third thing is, you say your whole life, "I want to sell this business." And then you realize you want something totally different once the time comes. So either way, all the achievements in the world are not going to bring you any closer to happiness. It's about figuring out what game you're playing. I think as an entrepreneur, you're like, "Okay, I'm gonna be successful. Okay, I'm gonna have nice cars, I'm gonna have an airplane and multiple houses," and you get all that shit, and you're like, "Fuck, I'm suffering even more now." And then you're just trying to protect what you've built. I'm 52 right now, so I'm at a different phase in my life, and I'm asking myself if this is the game I want to play for the next 20 years. So when I approach things that way, I am happy. It's really about helping other people and spending time with family.

I just took a four-day ski trip with my 12-year-old. We had four feet of fresh powder every day, and it was one of the best trips of my life. I think it's important to ask yourself, "What am I doing every day? Is this going to bring me more happiness?" When you start to hit midlife, something different happens. Some people get sober, some people get more fucked up. Some people dig into their relationships. Other people's relationships fail. You can change your job. You are looking at your life asking, "Why am I unhappy?" The tendency is to point the finger outward like it's your job's fault or your partner's fault. What I've done is face myself to say, "Okay, I'm going to take a deep look inside and figure out *how can I help my kids* and *how can I help others? How do I become a better partner and be more present with my family?"*

I think whatever your number is, you think you need so much more. I really didn't need as much monetarily as I thought I needed at one point in my life. In the suffering state, you project lack. When you are in a bountiful state, you see abundance and opportunity. To me, that's the magic of life—just being awake on the path and what you get to experience on the way. It's not so much about where you're going. It *is* all about the journey and who you need to become to get to where you want to go.

MARKUS KAULIUS

Markus Kaulius is the founder of Magnum Nutraceuticals and managing partner of Seven Ventures, the bestselling author of *Play a Bigger Game: Seven Universal Principles to Experience True Fulfillment and Win at Life* and has exited two multimillion-dollar businesses.

Markus and I were introduced somewhat randomly by a mutual friend, Randy Molland. Randy had a feeling Markus and I would hit it off—good call, Randy!

Markus is an eight-figure serial entrepreneur and the founder of Magnum Nutraceuticals and Seven Ventures Investment Corporation. Over his 25-plus year career, he grew his supplement company from a startup to $170 million and has helped clients worldwide lose over two million pounds. As a thought leader in the industry, he advises multiple eight, nine and ten-figure companies on growth strategy.

MARK FUJIWARA [MF]: How's life treating you? I get the sense things are going really well.

MARKUS KAULIUS [MK]: Life is going amazingly well right now. God has been so ridiculously generous and I might be feeling the best I've ever felt in my life. My book *Play a Bigger Game: Seven Universal Principles to Experience True Fulfillment and Win at Life* launched July 2024. Shortly after its launch, I found out that it was number 39 on the *USA Today* bestseller list. I showed my daughters while I was celebrating that achievement. My daughter looks at the list and she goes, "Dad, this is crazy. Number 40, I know this book. It's huge on TikTok. Your book is just as famous!" I'm just excited to put it in people's hands because they're simple principles. If you do them, it will radically change your life. Period.

MF: I wanted to thank you for your approach because one of the big things that I've started to realize is to let God take the lead. I was getting in the way of that. God gave me this gift

of hitting rock bottom through my mental health struggles. At that point in terms of healing, it's something as simple as "Listen to God." When things don't go right, I tend to ignore God or blame Him. From the day I met you, I remember you saying how God can do some beautiful things when you let Him do the work *for* you and *through* you.

MK: When you're about to do something spectacular—when God is going to do something spectacular through you—that's when the devil sends his best armies to come at you. If you were to look back on a movie of your life to see the best things that God ever did, you'd see they were after the devil's biggest attacks. I know why my wife and I are at each other lately—because I've got that big book thing next week. That's going to be huge. I look to God and I go, "God, I need you. I can't do anything alone. I'm not equipped enough to fight the devil by myself. All I have to do is invite you in and I know that. That doesn't mean all my problems are going to go away, but it means I'll have the strength to go to sleep and wake up tomorrow and do what you need me to do."

And Mark, this is the most important part: the minute we start getting derailed or getting off track, it's just…"Hey, you can get back on track right now. Right now. I don't care how far off the tracks you went." God is powerful enough to lift that train and go, "Boom!" You're right back on the tracks.

MF: That is so spot on. Recently, Amy [my wife] and I had this argument that really didn't need to happen. The devil gets so clever when we are on God's path. But when things are like this, just kinda coasting and we're doing well, the devil's really quiet.

MK: The whole bag of tricks comes out. And for my wife and I, we both 100 percent subscribe to this. We tell ourselves to be ready for whatever because the devil's coming to do his work. Now our car breaks down? Our cars don't ever break down, they're new. That's not right. We knew this was coming. As long as you know where that voice is coming from and you're prepared for it, you can invite God into it. "God, I know you'll give me the strength to get through this."

MF: And this is why I lean on my *ikigai*. It's why I called you. You are so authentic, you care, you want to have an impact. You've thought about this next mountain in your life. [Author David Brooks describes how people typically pursue individual success and achievement on the "first mountain" of life, but often later transition to the "second mountain" focused on deeper commitments to relationships, community service and moral purposes that transcend the self.]

It wasn't like you woke up one day and said, "Okay, I've got this money, now everything's fine." You've been really intentional about building this. Do you consider what you're doing now is at a higher level of purpose than what you were doing before?

MK: Yeah, well, thank you. It's just that God's been using the first 45 years to prepare me for what comes next. I don't yet know what that is. But that's okay with me. All I need to do is keep waking up and walking in faith each day.

MF: What do you think about this next life chapter that's happening for you?

MK: Well, there was a definitive moment for me. I think it might have been April 7 in 2022. I was in my car—I'll never forget it. I was in prayer and I heard God's clear voice say, "Your next chapter is about to start." Not only did I hear it, I felt it. After I heard this, there was just silence.

I was so excited for what I had heard and what might be coming and I asked him, "What is next? What will it be? What do you need from me?" His silence spoke volumes.

I could feel God telling me, "I have told you everything you need to know for now. You know what you need to do."

MF: Do you have an idea of what you're supposed to do?

MK: The very next day I came into work and I brought my

staff together and I said instinctively, "God spoke to me and the next chapter of my life is about to start. I don't know what it is. Here's what I do know: Tuesdays and Thursdays, I'll be upstairs in my office. I'm not here entirely for this business anymore. I'm gonna be praying until He tells me what I'm doing next."

And less than a week later, He said, "Write your book." I obeyed him and boom! I'm writing this book suddenly. I think a key part of it is a universal lesson for all of us: You don't need to know the exact next steps. God will often go, "Here's one step, are you going to take it?" To me, I love it because it's also faith in practice. I love when you don't have to pretend to know because God's got you.

So then I started writing this book. When it was getting close to the end, I started going, "Okay God, I'm about to finish the book and you haven't told me what comes next. I don't know anybody in this space, but I trust you."

Mark, I can't say for certain it was the same day but in my brain, it was the same day that I said that prayer that I got a message from an old Christian friend who said, "Hey, do you know who Rory Vaiden is? He is a Christian guy who makes books bestsellers."

I told him, "I was just praying about this." Then He introduces us. And it was so crystal clear.

You know those moments when Jesus shines a light and goes, "Hey, this is the path?" Rory was the path. He's put this beautiful veil on me. I love that because my ego can't get into it because I don't even fully understand. I don't. I have no idea what I'm doing tomorrow and I love it because all I have to do is keep walking in faith, which is where we started this conversation. Each day that I do it, I feel stronger in that strength of God's mind and then the generosity that He's pouring out on me is so ridiculous.

MF: This goes back to our role in life: to surrender, accept and release, right? Do you think this is more about keeping an open mind or just being in a receivership position with God?

MK: I don't think I've ever been a guy who prays for eight hours straight or something. But my idea of prayer is different from most people's. I have just an open conversation with God all day. I ask that God walk with me all day.

MF: God has led you down this beautiful path to tell you when to act. You told me about your exit in terms of the right timing, the right price and right terms. It couldn't have been more precise or perfect as it was. It seems like trusting God to lead you through your exit worked out well for you.

MK: Mark, He taught me this lesson so beautifully and it radically changed my wife and me. And the gifts that He gave us through this—unbelievable. So we moved into our dream home. This house is stunning. It is everything we ever dreamed of with the perfect view, the perfect pool, absolutely everything. He took care of the money in such a way that we had nothing to worry about to enjoy the house that was meant to be ours.

But wait, He goes, "I'm going to let you enjoy the house for what the house is. Maybe the craziest, most beautiful gift you've ever received." We just really enjoyed that in the moment.

We said, "Thank you for slowing us down. Thank you for letting us experience and actually enjoy this toy." Not, "Oh, that's a nice toy. Next toy, please."

MF: That keeps you present. Wow.

MK: I don't have to worry about tomorrow or the next year or the next day. I show up today. Here's my path for today and He will light up tomorrow's next step in the morning.

MF: Yeah, He's put you on a beautiful path and He'll continue to do so.

MK: When has He ever not? When has He given me a reason not to trust Him?

MF: Absolutely. When I have anxieties or when I have depression, it's typically when I'm listening to the devil or I'm trying to shut the noise off myself. I get in the way, even though I know this is the path right here in front of me.

These are times I feel myself going off His path to take my own path. And that's where all the stuff comes up, the insecurities and the doubts, the waking up at two in the morning, the rumination.

MK: Mark, you've heard me say this before, and you'll hear me say this a million more times. I am a one hundred percent believer that every challenge is actually a gift from God. So think about what you just said.

"That's when the anxiety kicks in, the depression kicks in. That's when I don't stay on the path properly."

Those are gifts. Why? Because they're notifications from God. He's showing us where to go, always. And He's showing you now.

MIKE KOENIGS

Mike Koenigs is the founder of Superpower Accelerator, the creator of the Life with Tesla documentary, a movie producer and leader of "You Everywhere Now," an organization helping entrepreneurs build their platforms and businesses. He has exited five multimillion-dollar businesses.

Mike and I spend time in a number of the same mastermind groups and at one point, we were part of this big entrepreneur group text where we'd share wins, challenges, memes and updates.

Mike is one of the first people I confided in about my addiction journey. He has become such a committed confidant that he even interrupted a beautiful meal in Paris to answer my phone call when I was at a particularly low point. I continue to be inspired by his willingness to help others in his circle. Mike has been dubbed an "Arsonist of The Mind" by Peter Diamandis who helps entrepreneurs create their "Next Act"—high net, low overhead, high impact, fewest moving parts, lifestyle-compatible businesses they love. A serial entrepreneur with five exits, a 19-time bestselling author and widely considered the secret weapon of hundreds of founders with whom he's crafted their "Next Act" using his Superpower Accelerator platform and system.

Before Mike came upon his true calling, despite his business successes, he realized that something was deeply wrong internally. His soul hurt; he was depressed and anxious. Quitting everything he didn't love, he did some deep transformational work that resulted in a new life. He realized that he'd been living out of alignment with his life's purpose.

MARK FUJIWARA [MF]: You planned this out [exiting]. It is so clear how aligned you are with your purpose. Each time I see you on stage—and you're on stage a lot—you light up more and more with each appearance. Because you're reaching higher and higher levels in that *ikigai*, to that dharma.

There's a good number of people who have this perception of exiting a business as this one big liquidity event. For example, I have a client with a medical company. He said, "I want to join the senior PGA, I'm going to golf with my buddies all day." Well, the problem is that you're 51 and all your buddies are still working. So they can only golf with you maybe once or twice a week. Now you're out playing with the old folks. He got so stressed and so depressed over his lack of an exit plan that he had a psychosomatic reaction when he got a skin condition that took a year to heal.

MIKE KOENIGS [MK]: Yeah, that is not uncommon. Every entrepreneur and business owner who exits has a period of time where they're fearful, anxious and even depressed after they sell what feels like their purpose and mission (their business) and don't know what to do next. I belong to a group called Ethos. It's a group of people where a lot of them are wealthy. They've had substantial exits themselves, eight-figure exits and above. There are a lot of them who are Burning Man regulars and what we all have in common is that we invested in this amazing experiential group.

MF: I can't tell you how honored I am that you're going to be part of this book. I am so impressed by the way you show up, your authenticity, your vulnerability. The way that you keep rising, not only with your *ikigai*, but with your impact. It lit me up when you talked to students recently. That was very powerful and I know it meant so much to you, too.

It was you talking openly about your first company, and how you didn't arrive at your exit just saying, "Oh, wow, now what?" You were very intentional about it. Is that something that's always been a part of your process or did something external influence you?

MK: If I am super clear on my journey as an entrepreneur, it has been and still is to a degree, fear-driven. I didn't know I had as much anxiety as I do—anxiety where I was just never comfortable in the world. I have what we now call a neurodiverse brain, severe ADHD. I don't think I'm on the spectrum, but I just didn't care about social norms. I didn't care about what someone would think of me. I did, but I didn't. I was afraid to create discomfort, social discomfort, by saying unusual things or strange things. The reason I think that's relevant is I learned how to code early on. I met some interesting creative people I felt a kinship to, who happened to be filmmakers. We started working on projects together and at the time I had a job. I'm very unemployable otherwise, but I had some cool people I worked with for a bit while I wrote video games.

Then these two guys and I started a company that became Digital Café [a new media company I co-founded]. Our intent was always to make enough money so we could make a movie. We never had enough money to make our movie because we didn't know how to run a business very well, but we were very creative and we got a lot of interesting projects. We ended up picking up clients like BMW, Sony and 20th Century Studios. We did some cool stuff including a branded video game called "Chex Quest" that shipped in six million boxes of cereal for General Mills. I was a good promoter and a good marketer. And I think my intent was always making money so we could exit and do what we really wanted to do, which was to make a movie.

By the time we finally got there, I was so burned out. When we made the movie, it cost a lot at the time, a chunk of my net worth and a lot of things went wrong. Then 9/11 happened, which decimated the film market. We got bypassed by the industry because we couldn't get screening and we couldn't get into any awards like Sundance. We made a calculated risk by shooting the movie in HD instead of film and there wasn't distribution yet! By the time we fixed our issues, the budget was long gone and the passion and desire to do it was long gone, too. I churned through a bunch of my net worth. I started working again and that eventually turned into my next set of businesses.

I'd say there's a certain degree of intention, but my drive has been to always get ahead, never fall back and never have to go back to the little town I came from. I think I had more fear of sliding down the pole and getting splinters in my ass. Then I was a lot more fearless of the future than the past. And that has been a constant drive.

MF: Would you say you started to go towards the path of what moved you to sell at the time?

MK: So again, if you look at going backward, writing video games was not a popular thing at the time. That turned into the equivalent of being a rock star in the present day. Back then, it was like, "What in the hell are you thinking? Why don't you get a real job?"

Then I got interested in marketing. I learned direct response marketing and started studying people like Dan Kennedy [a serial, multi-millionaire entrepreneur and marketing and business strategist] or some of the old classics to learn how to write copy. Because of my video and audio and production experience, along with my video game and development experience, we figured out how to hack the internet and websites. Before that, the only way to do multimedia was with CD-ROMs, or back then we used floppy disks to distribute our products.

That's how we promoted movies. I was always interested in whatever the next big thing was long before it was mainstream. I figured out how to commercialize it. I found business owner founders or division department heads who were willing to take a risk on the cutting edge and invest in our vision and give us the freedom to invent something.

So we invented new ways to market movies and even cars. We did some stuff for BMW. And then Sony, Columbia-Tristar, 20th Century Box. Anything you can imagine, computers, technology—3M was a client, Domino's Pizza was one.

I got involved with two technical companies that were software-assessed, two of the first that did automated marketing. We invented some of the first SaaS-based marketing platforms [software solutions hosted in the cloud and delivered to users over the internet on a subscription basis] for distributing video on the internet before *YouTube*. What drove me was I couldn't help but do what I did. It was like some sort of cutting-edge fascination. And I don't even think I was conscious of what I was doing—I just did it.

I found an unusual way to make a product that no one else had ever thought of and market and sell it and then talk about it. I think that's when I started discovering my voice and my ability to speak and teach and preach. If you fast forward, then I started speaking on stages and selling, which was another unusual set of skills. And then, basically internet, TV then podcasting. So we were definitely the first of the first doing those things when it was hard and really expensive.

Again, I can't honestly say I consciously did certain things on purpose. It was more like I couldn't help but do what I did. And it didn't really make that much sense at the time. What I was able to do was something no one else had thought of and no one else was doing. And if they were, I figured out a way to do it better and cheaper and faster to tell a better story and make it better.

MF: You spoke about something important earlier when you mentioned anxiety you experienced specifically as an entrepreneur. Did you have anxiety or any kind of mental health struggles growing up that may have also played a role?

MK: Yes, I did and still do. I was never diagnosed. I remember having crazy anxiety attacks that would freeze me up. But somehow, I learned to live in an imaginary world. It's a form of escapism that enables me to live outside of time and solve unusual challenges in the real world.

MF: It seems like that enabled you to imagine unusual things.

MK: That's what it turned into. I grew up in a little town in Minnesota where there was beer available to us when we were 12 or 13 years old. There'd be kids smoking some ditch weed, but I never wanted to have anything to do with that. When I was 18, I left home temporarily and went to a trade school where I met a kid who let me take a hit of weed, but I didn't know what I was doing. I had a very, very bad reaction and basically went nuts. I had what I know now to be an extraordinarily powerful anxiety attack.

To this day, if I touch any THC, I will wind up in the emergency room. I get a combination of murderous and suicidal, simultaneously. It's bad. I feel like I'm stuck in a loop of hell. I think by default, I'm able to be present enough to determine whether I am living in a state of heaven or hell, at least mentally. But when I smoke this stuff, I realize I just open up a gateway to hell and I can't close the gate. I am instantly surrounded by demonic forces and demonic thoughts. And as far as I know, I've always been there, it's just that I've been living in a little fantasy bubble. That's what it's like. I think when I look back, now I could be misremembering and it could have been a total hallucination.

I think that's what I experienced when I was a child and I'm not sure what triggered it. I think it used to happen regularly. I get occasionally triggered by cold weather, for example, which will cause a super negative reaction in my body. I hate being cold. That's one of a couple of things I will never do. Like people say, "Hey, I'm thinking about going to Everest."

And I'm like, "Why in the eff would you ever do something stupid like that? First of all, being up high where you die on rocks. That's like–you deserve it. And then secondly, dying of cold. What is wrong with you?"

In Minnesota, it was 35 below for two months. It sucks there. I would never, in a million years, ever want to go back. I hate it. Nothing about being cold appeals to my soul, my body or my brain. Part of it's because it triggers a bad reaction. It could be psychosomatic. I don't know what it is. I don't need to. Sunshine and waves, that is what turns me on.

MF: When you have these triggers, it sounds horrific. And

uncontrollable. What are the emotions that come up for you around this—sadness or even fear?

MK: It's like one of those things about panic attacks or fear of mental health issues. Here's what I do remember: when I was 18, I had this experience with weed that deeply affected me. I knew definitively what empathy for insanity or craziness was and for people going through that because I knew firsthand what it was like.

When you see people who are moving through some weird emotions on the street and walking strangely, or they're so OCD, they're walking over cracks. I've been there. I know that place. Your brain is telling you if you don't move in a certain synchronistic way or walk around some cracks, you're going to die or you're going to trigger some energetic event that destroys the universe, or some sort of crazy thing. I know that those things seem real to people with mental illness.

I have physically experienced it before and I've also observed it. I can feel it and I can put myself in that person's place pretty easily. I think the emotion—getting back to your original question—is pure terror. I think terror then can lead to despair if it feels like you'll never leave that place. Neither of those are nice feelings. I do everything I can to stay afloat. I suppose, on the one hand, you can embrace the anxiety or reject those emotions in their totality. I'll do everything I can to avoid them because I think they will consume and swallow me if I allow them to. I think that's where acting out in socially unacceptable ways, like unmanaged mental illness, leads to terrible things for me.

MF: Thanks for sharing that. It's very powerful. You've discovered that about yourself and then you've started to see the triggers, like physically being cold.

MK: I live in San Diego now and there's this illusion that it's warm here all the time. It's really not warm here all the time. It's like, if the 60s are warm to you? The ocean is in the 70s or something a few weeks a year. The Pacific Ocean is made of cold water. And if that doesn't sound cold enough to you, well, then spend a little time in it and you can't feel your toes after a couple minutes. But I'll swim in the winter. There was a year when I swam almost every day just to do it. And I did get used to it eventually. I think when I know I have control over it, it's a very different scenario than if I'm stuck. When you're going to a place for two months and you go outside and you're like, holy crap, 35 below is really cold. If you inhale with your mouth open, you'll actually hurt yourself. I'm thinking, this is dumb. This is a dumb place to live. I don't see any point in it at all. And then I remind myself that that's where my family is.

MF: Well, that's when you send them a plane ticket because it sucks when it's cold there.

MK: That's when I tell my family, "I love you. But don't get the two confused, me loving you and me going into a place that feels like hell. I want to be there for you, but it doesn't necessarily feel good to me. These things have nothing to do with one another." No, I'm all done. I do my cold plunge for two to five minutes a day. It's the worst thing that I do. I even look it up online, just at other people's times submerged but I don't want to do this at all.

I see the purpose in it, which is why I keep doing it because I think there is some value to doing it. The whole cold plunge thing is fairly controversial. You'll talk to people who will say, "There's no real hard scientific evidence proving that it's good for you or that it does something for your health." Now, is it good for mental fitness? Yeah. I think so. I think there's something to it. Can you build up a tolerance for it? I know you can go back and forth between these—hot sauna and a cold plunge —we used to do that up in northern Minnesota during the winter. When there was ice, we'd jump through the ice and then do the same thing in the sun and go back and forth five times and holy cow. I mean, talk about a detox.

MF: Yeah, it's called the Nordic Cycle.

MK: I think it's easy to make the intuitive leap and go, yep, there's something good about this. I remember not long ago, looking at some data that looked reasonably scientific that was saying, "Yeah, we don't know." So, if it makes you feel good, then I think that's great.

MF: With us talking about cold plunges, it reminds me that I'm in that space talking about these therapeutic modalities with others. Dan [my business coach] always takes me through all the latest health products to improve my mental health and energy. Do any of those stick out to you in your own practice?

MK: I'm really fortunate that I have a lot of clients in the longevity business. Recently, my friend, Steve Marlar, did an advanced body scan for me. He's located in Oklahoma City. At any given time, they have the highest quality and most recent full-body scanning equipment available. I think everyone from age 40 should get a full-body scan annually because we're at the same basic age where we have friends who are dropping like flies around us of preventable diseases. My best friend of many years, my business partner, found out he had prostate cancer and just went through a brand new treatment that did not involve lapping off his hoo-hoo and carving him up and then sewing it back in two years later and maybe...it's called "losing the angry inch." A lot of men don't know when they have prostate cancer. That's one of the choices: cut it off, carve you up and sew it back on. That's a bad deal.

Most diseases are preventable if they're scanned and detected early. And the time to do this is when you're 40, not when you're 50, or when you're symptomatic because by that point you're already effed. In my case, I was bleeding out of my butt, which was preventable by screening for colorectal cancer. I'm gonna tell you right now, getting your insides carved up is not fun and then going to chemo and radiation, not fun and completely preventable. The first sign of a heart attack is a heart attack. In my class of '63, of the kids that I went to school with, I think almost 15 of them are dead. And I'm 58 years old.

A lot of us grew up right in between or next to farms where they were pumping all sorts of chemicals into the fields in front of us and behind us. I know I used to run behind tractors spraying the fields, watching the bugs drop. And no one was stopping us kids from getting that harmful exposure. I wondered why maybe I got cancer and so did two of my friends who had colorectal cancer? With that in mind, I've been working with Reagan Archibald [founder of the peptide expert company East West Health] and several other experts with stem cells and nutritional supplements. I think right now, regular usage of peptides is a fantastic way to reverse early signs [of disease] and to get rid of pains by doing regeneration very, very safely.

Right now, the medical "disestablishment" and our government are making it increasingly difficult to get these treatments because there's a lot of money to be made. Thank you, OZEMPIC. There are billions, trillions at this stage of the game and they're doing everything they can to basically block the sale and then patent them by changing the molecules a little bit, then re-issuing them for thousands of dollars. Then they can charge the government and health care providers for a premium. But at this stage, the treatments are still really, really good.

I have been experimenting for five months on a carnivore diet, which means I eat primarily steaks. It sounds absolutely crazy that as a colorectal cancer survivor, I have half a colon, and half a rectum and I'm eating this way. I've had very, very difficult digestive issues ever since the surgery, but I found out a couple of things. As soon as I moved to an all-carnivore diet, I felt great and didn't have any gut issues. I found the biggest poison was seed oils. So canola, anything fried in that poison, that stuff is evil. Cut out every oil you can. And other than olive oil or beef tallow, for example, again, we've been lied to. That's the cause of high cholesterol. It's wild that I go on my pure carnivore diet, do quarterly bloodwork and I see that my triglyceride levels, my cholesterol levels dropped more than 20 percent when I went 100 percent carnivore. Everybody's different. For me, it's a lie—the whole "red meat is bad" is a lie. At least for me. I can't and won't speak for someone else's body or metabolism.

And then to be with my amazing wife. We tell each other everything. She's my best friend every minute as it passes by. I am very, very conscious of my mortality lately. On the one hand, that scares the hell out of me. But I treat every hour as though it's worth $10000 per hour, which helps me focus my energy on discerning how I earn and what I will spend my time doing.

I'll give you an example. This weekend, I was at a really, really amazing event, but there was a musical performer who was the most self-indulgent, narcissistic, "me, me, me" person. I just couldn't stand her energy. And I didn't like her voice, either. So I got up and I left.

Now someone might think, "Well, that's rude." I don't care. I don't let anything or anyone poison my brain. I don't care what anyone thinks. I will take care of the one thing I have control over and that's how I feel and how I think.

As far as my brain is concerned, I vet who and what I allow in, as in, "Who are you doing it with?"

MF: And "What are you doing? How's your mind? How's your brain? How's the energy around you?"

MK: Yeah, there's nothing selfish about taking care of you and not allowing poison inside your body or your brain or your soul.

MF: I think that's super powerful, too, and a lot of people don't realize they have that level of control. Because when you get rid of those people who are driving down your energy, that's when amazing things happen.

MK: That thinking gave me my own internal permission structure about six years ago. I realized I don't owe anyone an explanation. Unless we agree upon it first and someone's assumption about some social mores, that's their problem. It's not mine. And you don't owe anyone a response, a reaction. That's your energy. And if you're giving it away, you're allowing yourself to be stolen from. That's your sin. It's not theirs. That's your job. It's no one else's responsibility for every speck of energy you give away.

MF: I noticed it resonated at the top of the call when I talked about going through addiction leading me to this clarity about who I need to surround myself with. It's a good thing to ensure your circle gets smaller and more selective.

You knew in that hour, it didn't matter how good the music was, that the singer's energy was going to take you down. Especially when you say, "Okay, this moment is worth $10000," and you have other friends who have been passing away left and right. So you think, "How do I want to spend this hour now?" What does that look like for you overall?

MK: Yeah, you'll never get that time back. I think if you really, really get down to mental health, I'd say a good chunk [of it] has to do with self-value, self-worth. Now, some of it is clearly [caused by] bad chemicals that make you sad and unregulated, unmanaged mental fixations. There are all sorts of causes. I think I'm a lot more aware of my own now. And I think we all have them.

I'm now 58, and I'm much more conscious and aware of my sadness or anxiety. I know that they exist and what their source is.

I had a realization today. I was doing the self-exploratory meditation and I realized that for a big part of my life when I was feeling extreme anxiety, I'd have it because it was an escape in and of itself. I didn't use drugs or alcohol. I used anxiety as a temporary escape that had a beginning, a middle and an end, which got me out of a loop. I was like, holy cow, I can understand now what I call it, which is addiction. I don't know, but what I would say is I was using it completely unconsciously and being an unconscious partner in that cycle.

MF: It is like taking a substance, right? You want to get back to feeling something different and you take a substance to alter how you feel in the moment. But what you're talking about is not a substance, rather it's an action, though it's effectively doing the same thing.

MK: Yes. So getting back to the $10000 and where you invest

your time. I think a lot of self-worth and mental illness to some degree are driven by negative self-worth. Negative self-worth is the result of not learning how to value yourself or value your time or how to create value and be rewarded for it. Again, anytime I'm like, "Oh my God, I'm so broke. I'm not making enough," I go through the same thing. I'll be like, "Oh, I'm gonna run out. I'm not gonna have enough." I've got old, old programming running in my head that's not even mine. I'll be fine, but I still don't believe it. That's negative programming. But when I hear people talking about their inability to pay the bills, I'm like, "Well, that's because you're accepting a wage of $20 an hour or $25 an hour. You've never learned how to create value before. And that starts by valuing yourself and paying attention to what has value in your life."

MF: As I listen to you describe self-worth, I realize I haven't gone into much detail or depth with you about my addiction issues yet.

MK: Oh, no, you haven't.

MF: All of that was energy I took away from my family and all the money I spent. I've had issues with a borderline addiction to stimulants, too. But this online addiction was a lot more powerful to me, though.

MK: It all comes in different forms. We all have different judgments about what that means for us. 'Cause to someone else, they might look at that and go, "Yeah, I'll know how to stop, I'm no fool." But where does the guilt exist? Where was the intent to act? These are seeds that make addiction grow.

MF: It wasn't the best intent from me.

MK: I would argue, thank God, you have a rich person's addiction. I'm not trying to diminish any of it, but it's like, dude if we were living in a different time in the universe and people were having a conversation, they'd be like, "Yeah, so you're looking at a rock and it took too much of your time."

It's like in the grand scheme of things you could replace that and say, "Well, it's just like heroin," but I would argue, nope, it's a lot worse because it's more insidious, more concealable.

So many of us encounter addictive behaviors in ourselves. I'm just glad we recognized those for what they really are before they could wreak total havoc on our lives.

It's comforting to know how we can stay in control. We don't have to live like that anymore.

DAVID TRENT

David Trent is the founder and CEO of Trent Premier Growth and has exited two multimillion-dollar businesses. He is the bestselling author of *Elevate Others: Lessons for Purpose-Driven Entrepreneurs*.

I met David through a mastermind group, which was so helpful to me because he shared about exiting from his wealth management business. We often talk about working on our *ikigai* and how that translates into coaching others. David is a person I can talk to about anything without worrying about him approaching our conversation with an agenda. I've found that oftentimes in these groups, there is an underlying element of "Who can you refer me to?" David's approach is the complete opposite: he enters conversations by asking if he can offer resources.

His career in wealth management spans over 30 years, an experience that informs his work as a strategic growth coach to other entrepreneurs. He is an LXCouncil Certified Licensed Partner and CEO Group Leader, Certified Exit Planning Advisor and a Certified Pinnacle Guide. David lives an active life building communities and continuously growing his network of high-minded professionals.

MARK FUJIWARA [MF]: I recognize that some obvious pressures occur with a startup entrepreneur, especially a growth phase entrepreneur. But the most misunderstood entrepreneur is the exited entrepreneur. They have a lot of money, or they have *some* money at least, so there's not as much empathy for them. I've been in rooms before where exited entrepreneurs have opened up to where we're talking about suicides, potential suicides and panic attacks that get out of control. We're talking about mental health struggles that we all have that are exacerbated by not having a sense of identity, not having a purpose and feeling lonely.

You're someone who I look up to who has always been very

open with me. I feel like you have a lot to add to the conversation.

DAVID TRENT [DT]: Well, I hope so. I've seen enough people go through what you're talking about, so now I don't question it at all. I could see where it raises a lot of questions. Did they have some mental health issues as entrepreneurs? When they exited, there was a void there and they kind of lost their purpose, so to speak, so mental health kind of became more front and center.

MF: Yeah, so several of these people, some I've interviewed, were used to working eight to 12 hours a day. They were accustomed to being needed and had an obvious purpose, but then they saw how quickly those things got stripped away. The letdown after what you think is this big liquidity event—it has people feeling like they've come up short.

All the things they were looking forward to doing no longer seem so fulfilling. It's like, "Oh, this is all there is? This sucks. I feel like I've died while I'm still living." These people have too much idle time. When you get up to that level, you have all this time during the day because no one needs you anymore and it feels like your highest purpose is done. I'd say most people don't plan for that. They just plan for how they're going to spend the money, or how they're going to manage the money.

DT: You're pretty familiar with my situation. I don't need to work, but I knew that I wanted to coach, I just didn't know exactly what it would look like. I am an exit planner. I got certified in the business operating system world. That was the final piece that made everything make sense. I'm putting together CEO Roundtable groups. These are groups of 12 entrepreneurs. I intuitively knew that I wanted to keep pouring energy into people by coaching, mentoring and doing that kind of thing. That's where I get so much joy. I was ready to break from wealth management in the all-encompassing capacity I was in. I 'exited,' but I didn't *really* exit, like "I'm *done*, done," right?

I love capitalism. I want to make money. I'm having so much fun building something again. I just went into it from that standpoint. Now, I think I would be okay if I were just playing golf and traveling and doing that kind of thing. I don't think I would get to that low place mentally. I do think I would be less happy than I am right now, doing what I'm doing.

MF: Well, I think people are either a warning or an example, and you're an example. How was it that you continued forward, and was it almost a default reaction for you to keep moving? Did you have a plan at that point?

DT: I really can't say that I had a specific plan, but I had kind of a gut sense. I've just now gotten two coaching clients. And one is a young guy who's 38. He's an insurance agent. He's doing extremely well. He's going to do close to two million dollars in revenue this year, $800000 profit. He can keep growing, too. And he came to me and said, "I want you to coach me."

He's struggling because he's so driven. He's a good dad even when he didn't have a good experience with his father. Fortunately, his dad has become a great grandfather. He is struggling a little bit with turning the work mentally off at night, so we work through that kind of thing together. That's probably my best example of what drives me so much.

There's also a guy named Marlon Haines. He's 43-ish. I met him when he was 20, 22, when we sat down and talked about reading struggles for him and what his goals were.

He tells me this incredible story about how he was taught to be a victim, but that he just got it in his mind to get a degree. Now he's got a commercial janitorial company, enterprise value is probably $15 million. I sat down with him and told him about reading and the importance of that. I don't even remember doing this, but he says, "You showed me this list of 100 goals you had and you'd already achieved 75 of them."

That has become a lifelong friendship with him and he ended up coaching my son in basketball. He became like a second father or a big brother to my son, Carter. Working with that man for me is just the crucial life stuff, you know? You've had experiences like that around mental health and for me, I think this is innate because it's naturally what I love to do.

MF: We talked about purpose, *ikigai*, dharma. It sounds like you are living yours and it doesn't seem typical that people in your position feel like they always have a higher *ikigai*. They're always looking for something more, to no avail.

DT: I came across something today—I kind of go through these phases pulling inspiration from different books. I loved what I read this morning. It was, "Don't give your advice, *live* your advice." People get your message by watching you live it. I love that. I've got like, 33 things that I've tracked every day. I've put them in this B5 system that I've developed. I say develop when I mean it's repurposed, but it's "body, brain, bucks, being and bonds."

I've gotten to the point now where I'm just doing it to stay accountable with other people who keep track. I'm going to live what I preach. It's always with the Jim Rohn [entrepreneur, motivational speaker and author of *How to Obtain Wealth and Happiness*] caveat: "Listen to me carefully, but don't watch me too closely." Because I'm working on this stuff just as I'm telling you about it.

That needs to be at the forefront, and you're going to have awesome days and good days and hopefully most of them are either awesome or good. Then you're going to have that occasional day where you just know that wasn't my best day, but that's okay because you'll wake up tomorrow and go after it.

MF: You're similar to me in recognizing your unique ability with teaching, coaching and mentoring. The beauty of that is it's something that also lights you up from within, which I can see whenever we've had discussions about it. You're always driving for a higher purpose. You're also not like the typical wealth manager, by the way, who says, "Oh, I've reached my highest purpose, and it's working with these clients." But you've discovered what lights you up longer-term, and I'm guessing that it's something you've been very inten-tional about.

DT: I come back to these guys where I consume tons of their content, all of whom had a huge influence on me. And one that I've come back to recently is—do you know who Rob Dydrek is?

MF: Dydrek's awesome.

DT: Well, he's the guy that's like 80 percent of MTV's programming now, but he's got that [show] called *Ridiculousness*. But I mean, this guy has done extremely well. He has this deal where he looks at companies and he comes in as a 20 to 30 percent owner, trying to build companies that are of $50 to $150 million enterprise value, I think. He grew up in Michigan. He's a skateboarder. That's how his fame started when he was 14, 15. He was talented at it. He went pro when he was 15 or 16. But he's just a quirky dude. One of his sayings in his lower-down drawl is "perpetually evolving into his limitless potential."

MF: I love that.

DT: But he says it in a California way—he's a skateboarder. You get it. He's extremely funny and clever. I'd hate to be at a point where I go, "Why not my highest purpose? There's no such thing for me."

Dydrek also has a thing he calls his "rhythm of existence." He tracks everything he does and builds out this spreadsheet. So it's PILP, man. Perpetually Involved in the Limitless Potential.

MF: That's amazing. I've always sensed you are a student of this game yourself, in terms of trying to find better ways to perform well or trying to find better ways to show up to fill a role. I picked up my first Tony Robbins cassettes when I was 22 and it was always like, "Find the better way." I've carried that mindset with me for the entirety of my career.

There's also something so valuable about the consistency with which we live our daily lives. I've noticed how impactful it has been to form good habits in recovery specifically. It's all about getting the minimum effective dose for the maxi-mum effect.

DT: We have to apply that mindset with other things that are going to get you to self-mastery or perpetually evolving into your limitless potential.

All of this stuff works practically in our lives, not just in theory. We can choose vastness within our spirits, rather than constricting ourselves. There are overwhelming possibilities right on the other side of fear and self-limiting beliefs. We just need to be ready and willing to tap into our potential.

SIR DARREN JACKLIN (ROC)

Sir Darren Jacklin, ROC (Royal Order of Cappadocia) is a globally recognized entrepreneur, philanthropist and investor. As the Founder and Managing Director of Darren Jacklin Group of Companies Inc., he is strategically building a diversified portfolio of world-class companies and Multi-Family Real Estate Assets while spearheading the development of 100 LYNK Leadership Academy Schools worldwide.

After several insightful conversations that led me to be referred to Sir Darren Jacklin (ROC), I decided to finally meet him. I'm grateful I did because I quickly discovered that we share numerous values, ambitions and experiences. Sir Darren is a globally respected entrepreneur, investor and philanthropist with a remarkable ability to turn vision into reality.

What I find most inspiring about him is his relentless drive to create meaningful impact—whether through scaling businesses, acquiring companies or building 100 schools worldwide through the LYNK Foundation. His ability to challenge conventional thinking and bring innovative, purpose-driven strategies to every endeavor sets him apart.

As our friendship has grown organically, so has a strong foundation of mutual trust, respect, and collaboration, both professionally and personally.

MARK FUJIWARA [MF]: I know we've had previous conversations about developing a higher *ikigai*, a higher dharma after your first effort, then climbing farther. It's a beautiful metaphor in terms of your higher second mountain as you climb to success within your fulfillment. But I have to say that most people I know don't think about that.

Sir Darren Jacklin [DJ]: Most people don't even realize it.

I had the opportunity to debrief with a group of high-performing entrepreneurs who attended the event looking for a new kind of experience. I said, "Let's unpack this for a moment.

These are overachievers from all over North America, from all different industries—CEOs, entrepreneurs, executives, spanning multiple industries. But what does that make us? We're human *doings* rather than human *beings*—constantly hustling, grinding, chasing the next win. When you show up to the EQ [Emotional Intelligence] event, it's about who you are as a human being, not what you do. You slow down, you reconnect with yourself and others. Being out in nature removes distractions and creates space for real connection. It's an authentic bonding experience.

Here's something that is great for mental health: when you play pickleball, or you play golf or tennis or racquetball. It's fun as a competitive sport, but the thing is you don't really bond together because you're solo in it. I say, "I'm going to bring you to go hiking out in the wilderness."

The first thing your human brain thinks is of protection and survival: "Oh my gosh. What happens when we get eaten or attacked by a wild animal?" Instantly, we shift from independence to interdependence within the group.

Now, all of a sudden, we have to trust other people around us. Most high-achievers are used to operating solo, but in the wild we have to come together as a tribe, as a community.

Everybody in the group I formed did the hikes. We did three big hikes that day: group one, group two, group three. The first group started at 6:30 am, then 9 am, then 1 pm. And here's where it became powerful: we took all of that energy and connection to channel it into something bigger than ourselves. Our next move as a group is to build a school in Honduras. The concept is simple: "Take a Hike, Build a School." This shifts the group from attending a networking event to becoming part of a movement.

One guy on the hike was working on an $800 million real estate development. Another was managing a $40 million project in California. These are high-level players. But instead of sitting in a boardroom or paying tens of thousands for a consulting session, they spent hours side by side, walking, talking and sharing insights—building real relationships. At the end of the day, one of them walked up to me and said, "Can I give you a hug?" Now, neither of us are huggers, but in that moment, the connection was real.

He said, "I paid $250 to be here today. If I had hired that guy for a consultation, it would've cost me $30000. But instead, I just got two and a half hours of pure value on a hiking trail."

That's the power of shifting from transactional relationships to transformational experiences. And that's why we do what we do.

MF: This guy is doing an $800 million project. You saw his perspective shift right there in front of you.

DJ: When he was showing me what was possible, he looked at me and said, "You're playing way too small." And in that moment, he blew my mind. That's the part I love, just being around people who challenge me to expand my thinking, to level up.

One of the guys I brought to the event is working on a $40 million real estate project and he's struggling with his mental health. Loneliness has been a major challenge for him because his family doesn't fully support what he's doing. They see the risks he's taking and they don't understand his vision. That kind of isolation can be heavy.

I believe one of the best things we can do when we feel stuck is to get outside. Move—shift the energy. That's why my word for years has been "aliveness." Every single day, I'm tracking how I'm moving and what I'm doing to bring more aliveness in my actions. Because when you step into that mental space— when you embrace movement, adventure and human connection—then you're no longer just existing. You are fully alive.

MF: Wow. I want people to know your story, because you talk about aliveness and energy as well as your mental health,

which can go different ways once you've exited a business. I'm seeing two very close friends have their struggles becoming magnified as they exit their companies, because they didn't identify their purpose beforehand. They are finding they have too much time on their hands and their identity is gone. They're lonely and they don't know how to get out of that feeling.

Then there's your side, which is to go in the completely opposite direction. Correct me if I'm wrong, but you planned out your exit beforehand?

DJ: Yeah, absolutely. To add to what you just said: I had a guy who was from a prominent third-generation family, a very prominent family here in North America. They had just sold one of their companies. It took, what, three, four years to sell this company. When it was all said and done, after taxes, they were left with $150 million in liquid cash. A business that his grandfather started decades ago was now completely sold off because the third generation didn't want to continue running it.

The kids realized the third generation didn't want to keep running it, getting into the family dynamics and politics, so they decided to sell it all off. I told the principal, "You need to come to Vancouver."

He says, "Vancouver? What price do we need to come and be part of this?"

I explained, "It's not about the money. It's about showing up. It's about being in community, in collaboration with one another."

But when you're sitting on $100 million in cash, you probably feel pretty unstoppable. You might think you've got it all figured out. When he arrived, I gave him one simple rule: "Don't tell anyone who you are. Don't tell them about your lineage, or about the business and the money. Just be present." I told him, "Come up here because the LYNK Foundation is about elevating to educate. Come here to be part of something bigger."

Now, this guy has lived a privileged life. He's accustomed to private jets, luxury items at his disposal—he's never had to struggle. But here's the thing: when he came in with a low profile, under the radar, he didn't have to live under the weight of his name, his status or his wealth. He had the time of his life. Why? Because for the first time in a long time, nobody asked him for anything. Nobody tried to sell him anything or angle themselves for a deal. No one recognized his father's name, his grandfather's legacy or the billion-dollar business his family built. He was just a guy in nature, taking a hike.

MF: When you were in your company, before the liquidity event, did you have this picture in your mind of what you were going to do?

DJ: Absolutely. The idea came to me a couple years ago during a nighttime hike. I challenged myself to go on a solo trail hike and I thought, *What if I could replicate this feeling*? You don't have to go smoke marijuana or do drugs, you don't need to do Ayahuasca. There's just a natural state of being that provides clarity and allows you to be present. But what I was lacking was the infrastructure, having a team to run the day-to-day operations so we could create this experience at scale.

It's more than just a hike–it's like a mastermind group in motion. The powerful thing is that we're taking a hike and building a school. We're bringing together people from all walks of life. We've got high-achievers, entrepreneurs, executives, all individuals who have spent their entire lives chasing success. And I get it. I've been guilty of the same thing. I sacrificed my health to build financial wealth. Then I built the financial wealth and realized I had to go back to reclaim my health so that I could sustain it. So many people in business follow this same pattern. They grind, they hustle, they sacrifice their well-being to accumulate financial success, only to later find themselves spending their wealth trying to restore their health.

What I'm trying to do here is break that cycle. It's about creating an environment where people can grow, connect and contribute without having to compromise their well-being in the process. Because at the end of the day, real wealth isn't just about what's in your bank account. It's about your energy, vitality and the legacy you leave behind.

MF: That's right. So you were very intentional about that.

DJ: I was. I'll be 52 on August the fifth 9of 2025]. I'm always looking up to people in their 60s, 70s, 80s. When I was training for Mount Kilimanjaro last year in Vancouver, I had a gentleman who was 94 years of age humble me on the Grouse Grind in North Vancouver. I got to the top in an hour and five minutes. He was up there in 55 minutes. When I finally got up there, he turned to me and said, "What took you so long, young fella?" That moment stuck with me.

I introduced myself to him, thinking he must be in his 80s. When he told me he was 94, I was blown away. That's the kind of energy and longevity I want to model. So I'm always looking at people who are ahead of me. How do I learn from them? How do I shape my future to look like their present? And at the same time, I recognize that there is an entirely different perspective from younger generations in their 20s, 30s and 40s watching me in the same exact way. That's why I hold myself to such a high standard.

In 2022, I was knighted by The Royal Order of Cappadocia of Spain and became Sir Darren Jacklin (ROC). That title carries huge responsibility. I have people looking at me as a mentor and a leader, so I want to make sure I'm impeccable with my words because my words create my world.

MF: You hit upon something that is really near and dear to my heart, which is mentoring younger people. You have a limitless type of mindset when it comes to what you're doing right now and that's probably been the case all along with whatever you've put your mind to.

DJ: It's true. As a kid, I struggled with self-worth. I barely have a high school education. Growing up, I didn't believe I was smart enough, good enough or worthy enough to achieve big things. I used to go behind Staples and OfficeMax, take discarded boxes and I would cut out their logos—Microsoft, Kellogg's, Starbucks, Coca-Cola—plastering them all over my walls as motivation.

And then I would take sheets of paper, start with number 200 and count down to number one. I would write every reason why I was smart enough, good enough and worthy enough to one day train executives at these companies.

I had to rewire my internal belief system. Because, if I didn't believe in myself, how could I expect others to believe in me? That practice built my certainty over time. I knew that when I'd step into a room—whether with a CEO, an executive or an HR department—I'd be so confident, so sure of myself, that *they* would feel it.

I wrote about this in my book, *Until I Become: Purpose, Perseverance, Payoff.* As a kid, I was insecure—I just wanted to meet girls! So what I did was I used to take 10 Canadian pennies, put them in my left pocket and every time I'd say "Hello, good morning, good afternoon," I would transfer a penny from my left pocket to my right pocket secretly. The goal was to transfer 10 pennies from my left pocket to my right pocket. And then, when I started doing door-to-door knocking, door-to-door sales, selling different things throughout my life and then telemarketing, 400 phone calls a day, 2000 phone calls a week, I would always play this game with myself. It was all about conditioning myself to take action and build belief.

Two years ago, around Covid-19, I was the guest speaker on a Zoom video conference for a high-level business group. I was a key speaker at this event, but I had never met the guy who was introducing me. I logged on five minutes early and all of a sudden Zoom showed security updates, and then my MacBook Air had to do a restart. I was two or three minutes late getting on this call.

There's hundreds of successful business people on this Zoom

call. And Neil, the host, says, "Oh, Sir Darren Jacklin's here. Let's get started."

I very firmly said, "We need to stop. I need to acknowledge and apologize. I gave my word that I would be here on time and that did not happen. Some of you people are here right now, you read my biography, did some research on me and you're thinking, 'Wow, I want to meet this guy.' You're qualifying your time. Maybe you had to rearrange certain things with your family to be here. And I want to acknowledge that. I apologize for the impact of me not being here on time. Going forward, I've put together a structure that I'm going to test Zoom 15 minutes beforehand, put an alarm and a counter reminder with a notification. This is not going to happen again. Does anybody have anything they want to say?"

I waited for 60 seconds and no one said a word; it was uncomfortable. Neil said, "What a way to model integrity, of keeping your word," but I wasn't going to step over or out of integrity. Even though it's uncomfortable, I didn't want to do it. I was scared. I was nervous. I was uncomfortable. But I knew that integrity isn't about convenience, but consistency.

MF: I don't know many people who would be as direct as you were. I don't think many people realize what an effect it has when they do not respect other people's time.

DJ: Recently, I had a team member who kept showing up late to our calls. It wasn't just a one-time thing—it was becoming a pattern. And I know that when patterns show up, there's always something deeper at play.

When they signed on, I said, "Listen, can we just stop for a moment and let's just give presence to why you are always late? Let's go to the root cause. Let's not look at the tree, but at the root under the ground. What's the source of why you're always late like this?" So I started asking questions, bringing in another team member to create a space of curiosity without judgment. She says to me, "You know what it is, Darren, I feel like I don't matter. All my life I felt like I didn't matter." Wow. That was it.

It wasn't about time management. It wasn't about scheduling. It was something much deeper, something that had likely been ingrained in her since childhood. Now, how many people would take the time to call that out? Not in a way that shames, but in a way that liberates with kindness and in a safe space. It was about leading with the intention of helping someone break free from an unconscious pattern that had been holding them back. And that's the kind of leadership I believe in.

MF: So what I'm gathering is that everything you do in terms of making yourself a better version of yourself is ultimately through impacting others. You always have it in mind that you are a role model to this next generation, because you once felt that same apprehension about climbing the next mountain.

DJ: I've been watching something powerful play out in people. When I invite people into something new, like a sunrise hike, I see their mind-chatter start to kick in. They have an internal dialogue going on, comparing themselves to others. That's why I created a safe place for people where they feel accepted. They say, "I feel like I'm not being judged."

I called a friend recently who declined my invitation to hike. I asked him, "What's really the reason?"

He said, "Darren...you climb the biggest mountains in the world. You're training for Mount Everest Base Camp. Who am I? I could never keep up."

And I told him, "It's not a race. It's a beginner's hike. You belong. You matter." And that shifted everything for him.

You see, what's going on in here [points to the heart and the mind] is showing up out there—in your work, your relationships, your life.

We're here to take a look and do an inspection and look into your life. Where else does that show up in your life? The woman who showed up to the call late, the team member who said, "I don't matter." Where else does that show up in her life that she doesn't matter?

It shows up in all areas of her life and it's a blind spot. She doesn't see it. She's not present to that. She thinks she doesn't matter in life. She shows up to the top every day. She wakes up saying, "I don't matter. So if I show up late, I show up here anyway. I'm not committed. I'm kind of in and out, not really fully committed. I don't matter. I'm not going to commit to anything because I don't matter."

MF: And from your standpoint, what has gotten you to be the best version of yourself is that you know _you_ matter.

DJ: I know I'm good enough. Because I was always the kid who felt not good enough, being in special education. I've always been clumsy in sports. I was always picked last. And that's why it's inspiring now with all the hiking I'm doing, because people who have known me for years say, "Oh my gosh. You're doing _this_?" because they know me as I'm not "that guy," never that guy. It's honestly mind-blowing to them. It's a reminder to me and to them that we can rewrite our stories at any point. I am proof that the past doesn't define you and the way people see you doesn't have to limit your potential.

MF: Okay, let's go back to when you were growing up. I know it had to be tough. You're wanting to be accepted and you're always picked last. When did you feel a shift about how you saw your position or role in more positive ways?

DJ: I remember as a young kid being in special education elementary school and the Canadian Heart and Stroke Foundation came to our school where they did a presentation in our gymnasium for assembly. They had this competition where the kids could participate in going around the neighborhood, knocking on doors for the Jump Rope for Heart skipping competition. Kids got pledges through friends and family to give a financial donation to the Canadian Heart and Stroke Foundation.

Being the kid who was always labeled as the "dumbest" in class, the one no one thought could achieve anything, I decided to take a different approach. I didn't have the natural skills in physical education or sports like others did, but what I had was grit. I created a plan, set a goal and went to work. I knocked on thousands of doors over the next month. I didn't stop until I raised more money than all the teachers and students combined.

That was a turning point for me because in my mind, I knew that I was never going to be good at physical education or sports. But I could outwork everyone. Because whatever I lacked in skill, I made it up in numbers. My success was going to come from my hustle and relentless work ethic. I knew that if I knocked on enough doors, had enough conversations and put in the effort, I'd reach my target. That lesson, that feeling of proving everyone wrong, has stuck with me throughout my life.

MF: It really seems like you've capitalized on building on that formative experience when you were younger.

DJ: Yes, but for many years, I wasn't much of a team player. Then eight years ago, when Tatiana [my partner] came into my life, things changed. She was a high school senior teacher for 35 years, has three academic degrees and she's a huge team player. She modeled for me about creating teams and being a participating member on teams.

I've taken different training development courses. I did a rigorous one-year course for a team manager leadership program that transformed my life because I learned how to build up and work within teams. What I realized going through that program and through my own journaling was that most of my goals and dreams don't require my actions specifically.

If you look at Elon Musk or Richard Branson—these big people who are playing really big games in the world who have multiple companies, like Tony Robbins, who has over 100 companies. Most of his goals don't require his direct actions, because it's all about creating teams that run the day-to-day operations. I can stay high level as a visionary and have other people run the day-to-day operations. So most of my goals and dreams don't require my direct actions. That was a big turning point for me, because I've created over 7000 written goals for myself.

MF: Wait, how many, 7000? How often would you write these goals down?

DJ: I have my personal promises right here, Top 10. So for 30 years, I've made it a daily habit to read these top 10 goals every morning. Then every quarter, I review all my 7000 goals. When I go on an airplane, if I'm on a long flight, I put inspiring 80s music in my earbuds and I just go through all my 7000 goals, make edits and revisions and I'm constantly adding goals all the time. I had probably 10 to 20, 30 goals a week I set when I heard and saw people talk on social media. I'm always striving and I'm always achieving goals, as well.

MF: I love this idea, too, just because instead of having a lot of people say, "In X months or years, I will…" these could be something you could do next week. Or they could be small things that don't take a lot of time.

Is your process that you get inspired, then you write things down? Or do you keep it in a document you revisit often?

DJ: I have a whole master plan. I've had it made into a manual. I have a digitized version, as well, and it's a 250-year plan—yeah, three generations, wow. And I've spent probably 10000 hours, maybe $13000 on this thing. 15 minutes a day is 91.25 hours a year.

MF: When did you start this? Was it pretty early on in your career?

DJ: Yes, I'm 52 now. So that'd have been what, 17 years ago? Wow, I think it really started about 17 years ago.

MF: I write my goals out, too. Every time I have a setback or a visceral challenge, I rewrite them out again, just to continuously adjust and adapt my mindset to check things off as I achieve them.

DJ: I just recently started to do a thing called halftime adjustments. It's always from the first to the seventh of July every year. It's already on my calendar. So between July 1 and July 7, I review the first six months of the calendar year and look at my Top 10, what I call personal promises to myself. What do I give my promise to? It's like a standard. So then what I do is, from January to June, I look at my Top 10 personal promises and I say, "Do I need to make some adjustments?"

MF: This is so good. These personal promises, these 10 are your overarching goals in life?

DJ: These are the one-year goals. Then I look at halftime adjustments. It's half-over and it's kind of half-okay. So I take advantage of this week to plan out halftime adjustments. I ask myself, "Do any of these need adjustments? Are there areas I need to improve or places I need to pivot?" It's a practical way to recalibrate, refocus and ensure I'm staying on track with my goals.

I found there were things I needed to consolidate. For example, I noticed for the first six months of this year, I had a lot of separate breakfast, lunch and dinner meetings. So I realized, I'm committed to being in the best physical shape of my life. Why can't I invite others to join me? Now I can take those people hiking with me. I have the chance to spend one-on-one quality time with each person. When I connect in this way with other people, I am able to contribute to and enrich their lives. As people share what they're going through, I can then connect them with others in the group, fostering collaboration and network-building.

We're out in nature. We're physically exercising, increasing flexibility, range of motion, core strength, balance, breathing in great fresh air. When they return to their families, communities and teams, they're coming back with more energy, clarity and balance. That ripple effect extends to their respective circles and everyone benefits from that collective growth and connection.

It's not just about me anymore. It's about lifting up everyone around me.

MIKE MALATESTA

Mike Malatesta is a Dream Exit™ Expert Advisor and has exited two multimillion-dollar businesses.

Mike and I met through Justin Breen a few years ago when we connected on a Zoom call. We got to know each other better later on through the EpicFit mastermind I co-founded with Justin.

Mike thought he might go into coaching post-exit and specialize in selling your business and finding your purpose. He's developed a mindset built on designing a life driven by Options, rather than Obligations—to create new opportunities, relationships and success stories as a result of doing the things you most want to do while avoiding the things you don't. Mike's current Options include his Health, Family and new Business Adventure, ERC Midwest, LLC, the *How'd it Happen* podcast and the completion of his first book, all in addition to investing in startup companies. Mike's Dream Exit Playbook helps entrepreneurs plan for their exit to create maximum value for their businesses and prepare them for what's next in post-exited life.

MARK FUJIWARA [MF]: I know that you were in your business for quite a while. Then all of a sudden, you exited. Right after your exit, you start to discover your second mountain.

It seems like you were intentional about that. Because you already had in mind what you loved about the process and what your dharma or your *ikigai* were. Am I correct?

MIKE MALATESTA [MM]: Yes, largely. When I sold the first business, I think it helped me to work for the new company for a little while first, because I didn't think I was ready to leave all at once. I hadn't prepared myself as well as I could have. So that time that I was working with them gave me the time to think about what I wanted to be doing.

After that, it was much easier for me because I had that time to reflect and I also had time to transition out of the business on my own terms. Going from continuing to run the business to turning that over to someone else and working on special projects and then going to part-time, where I was only working a couple of days a week, gave me time to explore. When I was a Strategic Coach [a member of the Strategic Coach Membership Program], I had put together two decades' worth of goals and I had put together two decades' worth of goals for when I was 43 then 53 and then 63.

As I transitioned through, I was looking at these goals I had up on my wall thinking, *I sold this business so that I could go after some of these goals, but I haven't gone after them. So, am I serious about these, or is this just some exercise I did a long time ago?*

As I started exploring that, it started to accelerate because I started to meet people who were doing different things, you guys and other people, and all of a sudden, I was really narrowing in on where I thought I could be the most valuable to people. I was also narrowing in on doing things I liked doing, things that brought me energy. When I sold the second business, it was a whole different story. I was very, very prepared at that time.

MF: How long were you in both businesses?

MM: The first one was 22 years, give or take. And then the second one was around three-ish. So, you know, 25 plus or minus altogether.

MF: I think it really helps in terms of setting goals regularly, including where you want to be in a certain number of years. The other thing that I'm hearing from you is that you were intentional about sticking around and having more of a slower progression into your next phase. Am I correct in saying that and for what reasons were you moving in that way?

MM: Well, there were probably a number of reasons. But the one that I tell myself, which I believe is the most significant, is that when we sold the business, there was a big financial reason for me. It was a life point thing for me, but there was also this belief that this new company would create more opportunities. When we sold the business, I took that responsibility seriously and I wanted to make sure, to the extent that I could, that we delivered on the rationale we gave people. It wasn't just some BS like, "Hey, it's going to be great for everybody. I'll see you later. I hope it works out." It was more like, "I think this is going to be good for you, too. Here are the reasons why and I'm going to do my best to support that happening," which I think I did. It didn't work for everybody, but it certainly worked for more people than I probably could have made it work for on my own, if that makes sense.

That was the main reason, Mark, and the second one was probably that I wasn't ready to turn it over and I think this is one of the biggest issues that entrepreneurs struggle with. In my experience, they sell the business but they still want to own it. And that's a hard one. Whether you stay on or whether you don't, that can be a hard one if you don't have your head wrapped around letting go.

So I tried to tell myself before I sold it that once I sold it, whether I was going to stay on or not, my biggest responsibility was to make sure that we delivered on the promise to the team and that I did whatever I could to support the vision of the new owner. Because it's no longer mine and I think a lot of people really get stuck on that.

They get offended if someone changes part of the business or if someone doesn't listen to their idea and that can be hard. When you were making all the major decisions, at least they had to run things past you, you were very valuable, at least in your mind, right? But you may not be that afterward. So this was an important thing to reconcile for people because I've seen people struggle with that a great deal.

MF: You noted something important in terms of you

providing value. It's almost as if you knew that there was going to be a potentially difficult transition, so you didn't just rely on the fact that "Well, I'm going to have money and I can buy my happiness." Or you knew that there was inherent value in what you had to offer. There's this value that you've provided for 25-plus years that seems more dialed in now than ever.

MM: I always wanted to feel like I was doing something meaningful to me and someone else. There's a learning curve to that, too. There are all kinds of complications with some of the things I mentioned. You're used to making money. You're used to big checks coming in every two weeks or whatever and all of a sudden you're not getting that anymore. But you just got it in a lump sum and you sold the business. If you're used to it and that's how you value your contribution to your family or yourself or whatever, that can be a little tough, too.

There are all kinds of things. I don't think I've struggled from a mental health standpoint that much. I haven't, but that doesn't mean that I would suggest for a second that I had it all figured out, which is why I just think that's part of how I was built. I haven't had that part of the struggle. But maybe I haven't had that part of the struggle because of some of the intentionality of wrapping my head around stuff before I got into it. Well, I think that's a big deal because I feel like I've talked to some other people who have exited and didn't have that mindset.

To anyone who will listen or cares who is considering going through something like this sale of their business or whatever. I always tell them "The time to figure out what you're going to do isn't after the check comes, it's before if you can," and not everybody listens to that. A lot of people think that money will just solve every problem. Money only solves problems that money can solve, which is a lot. It's not like it's *not* valuable, but knowing who you are and having a sense of purpose about your life and creating value—however you define it—those aren't things that just pop up. Especially when you have the money to fall back on. It can be very easy to just keep putting it off and putting it off and spending money and going places and thinking, "Wow, this is great."

And if it is great, if that's exactly what gets you off now, I think that's fine. But I think for a lot of people, it's just a thing to do because that's what you're supposed to do.

They're sitting around thinking, "Man, I'm a lazy nobody now. And I can't say that to anybody. But that's how I feel."

You have to put on that mask saying "The world's great, man, because I just sold my company for a bunch of money and that must make me pretty damn special," no matter what I'm feeling.

As an entrepreneur or business owner, you're supposed to arrange your life so that you aren't needed. You're only needed for the highest level things, or for the things that you wanna do that just light you up all the time. That's what you're told. That's what a Strategic Coach tells you. That's what, I would say that that's like, a very, very small percentage of people. Most people are like, "This business needs me and I wanna be needed. Then I get to the point where I want to sell." So they sell. And then all of a sudden, they're sitting around, waiting for the kids to come home. It's amazing how fast nobody needs you anymore. And it's not that they fully don't need you anymore, it's that you've moved on and they have, too. They recognize that before you do.

MF: You know, the other thing, too, which is what you're doing right now with your project: helping the entrepreneur who's just *thinking* about selling. There's no price or due date. They're just thinking of selling to start considering the finances or how a team is going to be put together, which I think is so valuable—to consider how things are happening on the other side.

You thought about all of this in terms of the next half or the next step. It seems almost like when you thought about selling the company in the first place.

MM: Yeah, yeah. Well, like I said, I had those goals and that was always with me, even though I had first put them together quite a few years before, about six years before, but I had them. There aren't too many people who've been through an exercise like that, I guess, so maybe I had an advantage over more people because I had done some of that work and had never forgotten it. It was always in front of me. It's still always in front of me. I have it on my magnetic chalkboard. Even if the goals on their mark are not all the ones I came up with when I was 43, and I'm 58 now, I'm not going to do some of those goals anymore, but that's not the point. The point is that I've got a framework for thinking about my future and it's not because I sold a business that I sold my whole life. I just started a new one.

MF: Did you use any type of typical goal-setting model, like CAM [Clearly Stated, Achievable, Measurable], Vivid Vision, or anything like that or is it a list you always kept in front of you?

MM: Well, I was always a goal-setter. I became a better goal-setter when I went into it formally as a Strategic Coach, but I had always been a goal-setter. One of the things that I thought was the most valuable thing I could do was teach other people how to become goal-setters and goal-achievers, so we put a program together inside the business where we did just that. I tried to make everyone get into the habit of being goal-setters and goal-achievers. So, you know, of course, that works for some and it doesn't work for others because some people just aren't built for that.

Being a goal-setter helps for sure, but I think the biggest thing when it comes to exiting a business [is that] it's just very, very helpful to start thinking about your future before you sell the business or take the check.

And in my experience at least, that rarely happens beyond the big goal of selling the business. The typical, "Well, I'm going to travel, I'm going to play some golf, I'm going to get a place in Florida, I'm going to do this, I'm going to do that," all experiential stuff and [it's] probably all good to some extent. But like I said earlier, if that's not really what builds value in your life, then it's just things you're doing just because that's what you think you should do.

You can do better.

MIKE WANDLER

Mike Wandler is the president of L&H Industrial Inc., a third-generation, family-owned business.

My former mastermind co-founder introduced me to Mike and our very first conversation was an in-depth exchange about getting into flow and high consciousness.

In various ways, Mike embodies the Japanese way of building out a true legacy. He is not necessarily a classic exited entrepreneur—he will always be with the business and the business will always be with him.

Entering the family business at 14, Mike Wandler's road to entrepreneurship started without so much as a high school diploma. He quickly discovered the value of being self-directed and surrounding himself with like-minded individuals.

Coaching programs like Strategic Coach and 10x have helped him refine his leadership style, focus on his unique ability and delegate tasks effectively. Mike's emphasis is on building a company culture aligned with the values of its employees, vendors and customers, as well as the importance of achieving personal freedom and fulfillment alongside business success and the power of connecting with other entrepreneurs for support and mentorship.

Mike sees his journey as not just about business growth, but also about enhancing his overall quality of life and positively impacting those around him.

MARK FUJIWARA [MF]: I thought of you immediately when I started writing this book. One thing that came to mind is the misconception you've observed exited entrepreneurs have before they sell their companies. What have you noticed?

MW: I often see these mostly younger entrepreneurs assume this attitude that money will guarantee freedom. But the truth is you get more freedom *from* money, but only until you spend it, right? I think you lose freedom of purpose and relationships once money comes to the foreground.

MF: There was a guy I knew with $100 million in a company. About six months ago, he said, "I'll come to you when I sell my company."

I told him, "I don't want you to sell your company." This was after Blake and I had a lot of conversations around his exit struggles. I said, "I'm not going to help you sell your company until you tell me exactly what you're going to do afterwards. I want you to find a purpose that's as high if not higher than where you're at right now."

That's exactly it—what's your purpose? He called me up one day and he said, "I found it." He started a new company with one of his employees, which ended up being heart-centered, with a peer purpose. He was going to do a lot of work with inner city kids and buy a property to support them. So he flew me out to where he was, and we spent like seven hours together with his people, his three other owners.

I still don't think it's time for him to exit, though. The first thing out of his mouth when we were talking about selling his company was, "I built this company around the highest character people, these were like family and I'm not selling unless you and the buyer can guarantee that these people are going to stay on the board."

MW: Exactly. Matter of fact, I could assure you that a lot of them won't because it's a different person at the wheel.

MF: I think it's more about finding the right person with him in this case. I'm like, "Let's just find who to deal with as that outside person. That way, you can have full enjoyment, full *ikigai*, dharma, while doing your business. Then you can actually still do the same good."

MW: You do the stuff that's in your unique ability that you love to do, where you can be in flow. You take that other stuff and you find somebody you can delegate it to who would love to do that and would be in *their* flow by doing that particular job.

MF: That's exactly what we came across. Now, I brought a partner of mine out there to sell the company and to manage the assets. He realized the value and the purpose of the work. I also realized that it was what *he* wanted.

This scenario led me to see more clearly my unique ability in helping build communities of like-minded people, seeking companies with a high level of consciousness.

These are the same types of people I'm bringing to the table—entrepreneurs and practitioners alike, teaching the people with their own unique abilities who have built companies.

You've built your company around that same kind of intentional high consciousness.

MW: Seeing that unfold for entrepreneurs is very rare.

MF: One of my coaches, he built this company called Sage Wellness, which is an organic essential oil company that sold for $50 million. It's very similar to what you're doing because he realized that the employees were going in all these different directions. He brought in a couple coaches to be intentional about his exit by getting his staff's buy-in. Then he just says, "Whoever's on board with our mindset stays, whoever's not can leave." What he wanted was everyone to be on board in terms of the group consciousness. He got people to read the *Seven Spiritual Laws of Success* by Deepak Chopra. They started on a Sunday with the "Law of Potentiality" and read every single day.

In the next 12 months, he watched as his company doubled its growth, then doubled again, then doubled once more. This growth continued on like that for the next few years; every 12 to 18 months, it doubled. Then he exited on his terms, which was beautiful. He created a second mountain by helping others and collaborating with people who are doing the same thing on these different ventures.

Even with that kind of growth, does it seem to be lonely at the top for exited entrepreneurs?

MW: Yeah, it's as if you're above everybody else. You've got to make decisions that require you to not get too attached to anybody or anything. It's kind of a loner position. But then to do it right, you really have to truly care about everybody else, all your customers, all your vendors. It's lonely on top and you have to be okay with that. You have to be okay on your own. You've got to love yourself. You've got to know, "Here's why I get up. Here's what I do. Here are my unique abilities and that's what I bring to the party. And if it works, great. And if it doesn't, that's fine too. We'll just go." Everybody does their own thing.

MF: At one point I think we both agreed owners shouldn't be selling their companies so quickly. Are we on the same page with that idea?

MW: Full agreement. I've seen many people I went to Harvard with sell their companies and be unable to recreate them later. Then, they very quickly spent that money. Now we're not talking about hundreds of millions, but we're still talking about $10 to $30 million. They sold their companies because they decided they didn't like the company they were in as it was, which I can easily see happening.

If you don't like what you're doing as a company, change it. Ones that sold it in order to change it literally weren't able to recreate a new one and had to go to work for some of the other entrepreneurs I know, which is a nightmare. If you've been an entrepreneur and you had the taste of those entrepreneurial freedoms and then have to work for somebody else, it's a nightmare for you because you've tasted the other side of it.

I like how Warren Buffett—and a lot of the people in Japan and China—won't sell businesses with the intent to keep them running indefinitely. They're also not ever thinking about selling their businesses for immediate gain. I like that better. But I'm fine with selling it. If you're no longer interested in the direction things are going, if you don't want to do that anymore, fine. That's the right time to figure out *how* to exit it. But that's kind of too late to get your premium if I'm being honest.

If you're not really in the game, but you're setting your business up with a Strategic Coach, then you are trying to set your business up for a big payday. To me, that is not interesting at all. I'm like, "No, I want to set one up that's going to keep going in the future." When opportunities come up, when the new fad comes up and you can jump on it, you can make a bunch of money with it pretty quickly. That's not very interesting to me because I like my work to continue expanding. I do think that if you get tired of a piece of your business, there's a time to sell it off and get rid of it or to just shut it down. But the entire business, it's a real ecosystem with this tribe of people. And I'm kind of into this tribe of people running at like 150 people. I can run 150 people and then each one of them can run another 150 people, which ends up being 22500 people, I believe, in just two layers.

You could scale out very quickly. A tribe of 150 people should be carefully curated using all the tools you have in Strategic Coach that help you find the right people to get them in where they can apply their unique abilities. Get them to that Michael Jordan operational level, get them into flow with the team and then go find what the world needs that you could provide. The team could then make enough money to keep the business going until the world no longer needs what they are creating or selling.

Then move on to the next thing. I think that's the coolest thing to do and I think that's what Warren Buffett has done. I think that's what a lot of really long-term successful companies have done. They set up that tribe and then when people leave, somebody else comes in and probably elevates the tribe if it's set up correctly. Not necessarily true, though, in professional sports. The Chicago Bulls didn't keep getting better and better after Jordan, but I think it's a worthy goal.

Nationally and internationally we've got 400, 500 people running under the L&H logo. That presence of hundreds of employees affects another triple that many people, between customers and vendors and family. So you've got thousands of people who are positively affected and if you can get them in flow, well that's how you create that high consciousness in a sustainable way.

It's really about getting those tribes into mental fitness up through flow. Becoming really unstoppable and you're creating heaven on earth for as many people in those tribes as who want to participate. You're going to have people in those tribes who don't buy into this stuff, which is fine. We can probably find a place for them. The leaders, in order to orchestrate team flow, have to be practicing all of these things personally. And I think that's where I'm headed.

Now, I'm not seeing the doubling in sales like your friend was seeing. I don't know why. But there is growth and I'm happy to see that.

MF: He was in a business that was very niche and it was a product at the time that was very, very unique. There were stages of organic essential oils. This is up in Canada. So I feel like what he was achieving or where he was on a high level, the risk was high as well. With L&H, you're maximizing the risk/return. It's interesting that your peer purpose plays out here. I can see how that progresses.

MW: I've spent a lot of time around these people who are doing their business just to sell it. As quickly as possible, really, for as much money as possible. And it always confused me. But for years, I didn't understand why it confused me. And now, as I've done all of this mental fitness, it's become clear to me. So I ask them, "Why do you want to sell your business?" I tell them what I told you, which is that a lot of entrepreneurs I've seen sell their business are miserable because they couldn't recreate it and retire. With all of those preachings, retirement's really not even very exciting to me. Now, I don't want to be doing what I'm doing right now forever, so I'll change and morph just like I always have.

Once I get to master something, then I can put that aside. I will then try something else more challenging. To stay in flow, you have to always be challenging yourself a little bit more, five percent more of a challenge to get into flow.

By design, I'm always going to be doing something different and I want to work less as I get older. But all of that gets fed by this life's purpose, a massively transformative purpose that I'm headed towards that'll never end. It might update or improve, but it won't end. You do it until you can't do it anymore—and by then, you're hopefully within a few hours of death.

MF: That's the way it really should be. I was at an impromptu mastermind group a few months ago where the exited entrepreneurs were ranging anywhere from $20 million on up to close to $200 million. I decided to share about some of my struggles.

Before I could even finish my sentence, everybody in the room started raising their hands. There was one couple where the husband and wife ran the company together. They sold it for about $60 million. They told the group, "We've never been more lonely in our lives. We've never been more sad, we don't have direction, we don't have purpose and we've discovered who our true friends are the hard way." They said they didn't have anybody in their circle who would understand if they said, "Hey we're depressed."

Most everyone was sharing the same kind of story and feelings. Some had built second mountains but it wasn't quite as high as the first one.

To your earlier point there, that's kind of like the American dream, except it's incomplete.

MW: That's the entrepreneur dream, right? Yeah.

MF: There are not a lot of people we meet who say, "Well, I'm going to start this company and I'm going to run it until the day I die."

MW: Because it feels like a life sentence to them. Because it is. But you turn that around and you say, "Well, I'm not saying you have to work 50, 60 hours a week and make every decision and do a bunch of stuff that you don't like doing that is not within your unique abilities to do." But owning it and being the CEO or the Chairman of the Board and then hiring people to do everything you don't want to do, that's the idea. The trick is to hire some really good people who love doing it and are amazing at it and it gets them in flow. My job as owner, I own 50 percent of L&H and my son and two nephews own the other 50 percent. Having it privately held is a real blessing. So much so that it actually took us 60 years to gather it up.

We just finished this year gathering up 100 percent of it in the family. That's really amazing because we have to personally be accountable to the bank. I've got about $40 million with the bank, but other than that, we're not accountable to anybody else. We don't have to ask anybody about what we want to do. And that's beautiful. Then if we don't like our company or what we're doing, shame on us because we can just change it. I hear my guys saying things like, "Well, this rule we got, this is a stupid rule." Okay, well, we made the rule, we can change it. Should we change it?

MF: That's the right conversation. Exactly.

MW: We can literally change it in two minutes. If we've made some stupid rule, we'll just freaking change it. If it's not serving our people or we've made a mistake, no problem. We get to set it up exactly how we want to perpetually, then morph it to meet our customers' needs. Really the only scary part of that is, okay, what if all the work goes away and we go bankrupt?

Now, that's technically always a possibility. We've been at this for 60 years and we haven't yet. If we keep ourselves together and we stay in good markets and we stay diversified enough, we mitigate a lot of those risks.

I do think there's a massive amount of emotional risk in what you're saying, which is that "If I were to sell this, I'm going to be miserable. I'm going to have a lot of money, but I'm going to be miserable because this is my baby and I love doing it. All of my employees and all of my customers and all of my vendors are going to suffer because I am pushing the reset button."

It's kind of like a couple getting divorced. The kids might have trauma for the rest of their lives, dealing with that crap. The reality is, most of these companies don't survive being sold. They just get ripped up and tossed in the air.

I think it's a lot more cool to foundationally set it up to perpetually feed this tribe of people who collectively are doing wonderful work already. If the people aren't doing wonderful work, then it inevitably implodes, which it should. You teach them how to get into flow, which is why I wrote my book *Know Thyself, Love Thyself: A Practical Roadmap for Optimizing Performance through Mental Fitness, Cultivating Healthy Relationships and Creating your own Heaven on Earth* and I'm leaving the record of how to do it.

If you do that, I think to your point, the sky's the limit. You might not be doubling growth every year because you're a little bit risk-averse or you're in a market with a lot of competition, but you'll still grow. Most people suck comparatively because they don't get it and they're not in it for the long run.

It's also why I'm getting a seat at the table with all of these big nuclear companies and all of these huge customers that need energy because we've been in it for 60 years and we know how to make things and we know how to fix things and we love doing both.

MF: It's a well-oiled machine that works when you need it to, right?

MW: That's right. It gives you a seat at the table for the next big thing and there will never not be another big thing. Humans figure out the next problem, then the problem after that shows up.

MF: I think that the message of putting yourself in flow as much as possible, having your people do the same thing, is really important.

I've also learned to seek out things that I love doing—*ikigai*—outside of business that get me into flow as quickly as possible. That's the reason why I do archery. Then just recently my

wife got me these one-on-one lessons with one of the best Japanese calligraphy instructors directly from Japan. Calligraphy is a science and it's about being in the present, breathing. It's meditative. The discipline is achieving muscle memory to set ink to paper. The meditation consists of writing and creating these unique characters with one movement, one breath.

The clearer your mind, the more beautiful the stroke is. She's teaching me how to do *kanji*. It's this beautiful exercise that we get to do every Saturday. It's a skill where I'm always seeking to perfect it, but I'll never attain that level of mastery completely, which keeps me in that flow state. It's in the striving, in the effort for me.

MW: You're pushing five percent harder and dropping into flow. Exactly. You have to be out of your comfort zone to get into that flow. That's why once we master something, we move on to something else because we've perfected that one skill. The discomfort is where our growth applies.

"Okay, what's next?" Which is great and wonderful to always ask yourself.

Some people will say, "Well, that's just greedy," or whatever. Never be contained.

MF: Same thing in our businesses.

MW: You are acting as if you are new and perpetually learning.

MF: Right. One of the things I've observed as I am building intentional communities of exited entrepreneurs is the need to draw deeper into ourselves as individuals for the betterment of the group. What's really interesting is when I introduce others to Internal Family System (IFS) work, which has been so instrumental in my individual growth.

One of my business coaches is amazing at practicing it and it's uncovered a lot of obstacles that have affected my life significantly, yet unconsciously. Doing an IFS exercise means

getting to the heart of those emotions stemming back to something you experienced in early childhood.

For me to do one-on-one with my coach here, that's incredible. But what if you have a small group like a mastermind,
practicing IFS together? I've seen my coach do it with other
clients in a small group. And even though we might have
different childhood experiences or traumas, we learn how to
activate those same emotions in a healthy way. It's incredibly
powerful to see things through somebody else's eyes while
learning about their lived experiences.

MW: I think that it's helpful to know that everybody has those
emotions and that there are ways to let them go. I really welcome
it. I learned how to do that at "40 Years of Zen," [an immersive
neurofeedback training and education to unlock potential] with
my facilitator, Travis. I learned how to look for those trigger
moments when I know that something's really making my blood
boil or making my neck tense because I've dealt with something
similar in the past. Now I say, "I'm gonna sit in this feeling and
I'm gonna try to sit in it long enough to have it expose itself." It's
about making the unconscious conscious.

This is also why I decided to do the psilocybin trip with
Travis—to kick the doors open and try to see my mind differently. He thought there was something bigger and grander there
than there was. We didn't find anything ultimately, but the trip
was amazing, absolutely life-changing. I see that I used to run
away from those tensions and those traumatic things that came
to the surface for me. Now I run right towards them, which was
one thing that I needed to learn how to do. That's happening
regularly in my life now and it's wonderful.

It's a superpower to share this human side of ourselves with
other people. As a matter of fact, we're all creating patterns
every day based on past trauma, whether we have external triggers or not. You can reset it and you can get rid of it or reframe it
if you want, there are so many ways to change your mindset.

Somebody like Travis or a coach can help you figure out your way. I consider these self-discoveries to be a superpower. It makes life so fun, because even the tense, uncomfortable stuff becomes interesting. I always tell my tribe that a trigger is really just an opportunity.

Then there's the resilience you build. It is certain you're going to have tragedy, death, grief, fear, anger, addiction that knocks you down to those lower levels of vibration. The mental resilience builds up by regularly asking yourself "How long are you going to spend down there before you come back up?" You're not immune to being down in that place–none of us are. You're going to get punched in the face. But how long does it take before you come back up to your normal state or baseline? And that brings up another point of choosing where your normal state is, where your default vibration level is.

Your level of joy is a choice that you predetermine, that you preset at some time in your past. But the good thing is that you can change it to go up or down. The fact that it's a choice is something that other people don't know, and they need to know that. People need to know they're choosing their level of joy, or their level of vibration, their default position. Knowing all of this also makes me very judgy of people. My wife feels judged some-times when I remind her about it. She knows that she went to the same class as I did. I'm just stating the truth. But I know it's judgy of me.

MF: Well, I think a lot of us tend to put a ceiling on our vibrational levels. It's self-limiting.

MW: Yeah, we don't allow ourselves to go higher than that.

MF: It's like, "Well, this is good enough."

MW: If you consciously make that choice that you want to be vibrating at this level, or even if you want to be down here in hell in fear and grief and misery, you can stay, so long as you know it's a choice. Now I'm going to choose not to play with you, not to work with you, not to be married to you and not to spend a lot of time with you. If you're family, sure, you know,

I'm not going to lose my shit if we've got to go to a wedding, a funeral or something and spend a little bit of time together as a family. But I'm also not going to carve out a week to go stay with you if you choose to vibrate at a low level, because it's not what *I* want to do. I think that's all true and complicated, which is why it's a practice.

MF: Yes, and it's a practice that can really help within an entire family system. I feel like you can set your intentions of remaining at your default vibrational energy rather than going down a level, but it takes effort. Over a sustained period, that is a bunch of energy and effort that you're outputting. I feel like that's the better way to go, but it is also tiring.

MW: I have a couple thoughts on that. First, the thing that causes exhaustion is feeling the effects of the fact that you are who you hang out with. The second thing is, as I've been able to really practice my level of vibration and sustain it up at a higher level, then I can change the vibe of the whole room. Because people are talking about how this one person is just always a bummer. But whenever I run into them, they're not a bummer, they're fine. You know, we have amazing conversations. And I figured out through studying and through talking to people that it's because I'm becoming really strong in my own personal vibrational level.

The room always goes to whoever has the highest level of commitment and the most practice in their vibrational level. If I come up against my ex-father-in-law, he's pretty committed. He's spent his whole life at this low level of vibration, just nastiness. But even now, I believe if you've both spent the same amount of time in your respective levels, and you're both as committed, and you're one vibration level here and one there, the higher one wins if everything else is equal. But if this person is more committed and more practiced being at their lower level, then it will pull you down to where they are.

I also know that I don't want to hang out with these people at a low level of vibration. That's not who I'm trying to be. What you're doing is curating this tribe that all vibrates at this really high level so we can go further together in the same direction. I give people in my tribe the knowledge that there's a choice, that they're making choices and then curate the tribe to be at a higher level while practicing growing together. I think it'll be unstoppable and it will continue growth for the team at one percent a day.

MF: For continuous improvement, one percent a day.

MW: Man, after a year, that compounding interest is tremendous. After 10 years, it's mind-blowing.

MF: One percent a day or one percent a week is good enough, right?

MW: Exactly. Always practicing and always learning and improving. It's all very personal. People go through divorces, they go through addiction and they have their tough times. You don't cut them loose just because they've had a bad moment. Like with a divorce, we usually give people six months to get their heads out of their asses and then we'll have conversations about it.

It takes people time to go through stuff. To some degree, it depends on the level of performance. I encourage people to keep working with coaches like Travis for when inevitable friction happens. If their way of dealing with a crisis is to say, "Oh, I'll sit on the couch," there's another crisis building right then and there.

MF: That's right.

MW: Your immunity to crises is all of these other levels above combined: mental resilience, unique ability, mission, vision, values, flow. That's your immunity to crises.

MF: I think if we're all desiring to be in flow at all times, where we are willing to work on this individually, we will spend less time in the lower levels. It is natural to dip, but you start to see fewer instances that take you out of flow. Working on all of these things that include noticing a reaction and identifying it to recognize that pattern keeping you away from

flow, instead of just succumbing to our default attitudes automatically. Or, as you just mentioned, too, approaching a new obstacle, but not letting that take you out of flow. It takes a lot of energy to do both.

MW: And then if you're running away, you always feel bad. Or if you're avoiding it, you always feel bad. If you just walk up to the conflict or obstacle to say, "Hey, let's work on this," then you don't feel bad in the long run. Even if you don't succeed immediately, you don't have to be saddled with that bad feeling that comes with avoiding conflict in the first place. You always have the choice to be brave.

DR. DENISE BROWN

Dr. Denise Brown is a partner and management consultant at Sage Partners. As CEO, she led the sale of the virtual health company, Fident Health. She has over 20 years' experience as a business and clinical leader at Vituity, a physician-led healthcare organization.

I met Denise through a mastermind. I value her experience as both a clinician and an exited entrepreneur. She has decades worth of experience working with patients to deepen the benefits of integrative medicine. She coaches other medical staff as well as entrepreneurs on priority management, curating a well-balanced life and learning to cultivate contentment, both professionally and personally. She has served as Medical Director and Vice President of Practice Development at Vituity Physician Partnership & Healthcare Staffing Solutions and Hospital Medical Director at Sequoia Hospital in Redwood City, California.

MARK FUJIWARA [MF]: How long were you at your company before you exited?

DR. DENISE BROWN [DB]: It was more like a gestational period than anything. They brought me on in November of '22 and we ended up closing at the end of September '23. It really was kind of a 10-month whirlwind with the most recent iteration of the company. I think maybe now, looking back on it, I want to believe it gave me some objectivity on the matter. But at that moment, I wasn't feeling terribly objective.

MF: And from that point to when the company was sold, how long was that until they told you?

DB: Oh, it was less than three months. We went from May to September. I think it was a combination of a lot of things and I still struggle with this, but I won't say I suffer from this. I did the right thing and I was mad because I would have made different decisions had I known all of the information up front. If I had known that this was the direction we were going, I would have done things differently. I don't like feeling as if I didn't do the best job possible. And then it turns out that it's all in my head. It's not actually true at all, because what I ended up doing is the reason that the company was able to go for sale when it did. But at the time, it made me second-guess a lot of the things that I had done, and I am not a person who second-guesses myself very often. That was weird and unusual for me. Then I was questioning my decision-making, which is not a normal thing for me, either. Both of those things were probably good to learn from, though.

MF: So then it suddenly ends. What was it like when your business got sold?

DB: I think the closest thing to what I could call it was a grief reaction. I was almost angry. I knew that we were on track to do even bigger things. And I had sort of been brought on with the idea that we would not even put it out there until maybe the fall of '25. I thought I had at least three years to prepare, but then I understand things happen—someone was interested and who's going to say no? I was brought in by private equity and I thought to myself, *If you had told me this up front, then we would need a turnaround person in place.* Knowing it was less than a year, I'm not convinced I would have left my previous engagement because that's not where I planned to go.

MF: Right.

DB: The position was billed in a way that claimed "We want your growth expertise, we're looking for explosive growth," blah, blah. I knew that was exactly what I'm good at and enjoy doing. So I was angry at first. Now, with a little bit of hindsight, I actually think it was a great thing that happened. It was a super formative learning experience for me. I eventually decided I had to deal with it like I would stages of grief, and that was the only way I was going to get through those difficult feelings. Now I guess apparently I've entered my acceptance phase.

MF: I love that you processed your exit like stages of grief. When did you start thinking of it as a process in general?

DB: It was almost immediately when I conceded, "Well, they were looking for investors." Then I thought, *Well, sure, everyone's always looking for investors.* I have no problem talking to anybody or asking people for money. That doesn't bother me.

But then it became clear to me that no one wanted to just come out and say, "We should sell it." I felt like I should have been at least part of that conversation. I get that it's a portfolio company, but that didn't sit well. I was angry most of the month of May and probably part of June.

Then I went into full-on depression mode where I kept repeating to myself, "I can't believe this is happening," which really lingered internally.

I was excited that it was for sale and there were all of those great things that come with that kind of success. Those things were all well and good, but they were tempered with thoughts like, *If you guys would have just let me run with this for 18 more months, we could have all made out so much better.* At the time, I was still second-guessing my choices.

When it all ended, I wasn't thrilled with who bought the company because I knew that all of the work we had done and all of this transformation we had achieved was just going to get filed in their realm file, you know what I mean?

So it felt like a waste of time. Then I got mad about that, too. I'm fuming about it, thinking, *Oh man, I didn't need to pick this one. I could have picked something else.* Eventually you have to let go of it. I think in terms of the stages of grief, it's anger and then "I don't want to get out of bed." Then it's finally like, "Y'all have reserved the right to make terrible decisions."

MF: Can you tell me how this was different from typical feelings of depression? I actually have times where I do get angry but I keep it inside. Freud said something like "Depression is anger turned inward"—it's like that for me. I deal with grief the same way you do, but I have external episodes where the anger is not from something traumatic, it just exists.

DB: I think most of my depression is really around loss. I wouldn't say I'm an inherently depressed person, except when I lost my mom pretty early in medical school—I was 24. I never really had a chance or the opportunity to deal with any of that properly because I had to keep going with my residency. I think I had a lot of unresolved grief by not processing that loss. In this case, the sale was happening as my older kid was going off to college. Things compounded as I put them on the back burner for 20 years, because I didn't have time to deal with grief in the way I needed to.

I already would have been sad about my kid heading off to school, but the timing just unmasked and amplified that, because it felt like yet another loss on top of previous loss.

Everyone was running around celebrating [the exit], which was great. Yes, I am very excited that this happened and aren't I fortunate? So I don't mean to look a gift horse in the mouth, but at the same time it really was a loss for me. It's something that you've poured all or most of your energy into and I don't think it's unreasonable to look at it like a loss. It became part of this whole unresolved grief that I was dealing with already. I had never actually seen a therapist or anything like that because I was sadly brought up in the school of "Shut up and get on with it." I did finally start seeing someone and she was the one who said, "Well, it seems like there's all these little losses that are stacking up." That was actually helpful to chat about.

I know you and I briefly mentioned this when we talked the last time, but it really wasn't until I did this oral ketamine stuff that I finally let it all go. It took me that experience to let go and the guide kept asking, "What are you grieving?" And I said, "Well, I think I'm grieving a lot of things, but let's just call it grief with a capital G." The healing process from that—I don't know that it necessarily matters what the individual little occurrences were, and that's what I'm trying to figure out: how to knit myself together differently. That was super effective. That process actually has helped so much, so I know what it's worth.

MF: That brings up another part of our last conversation when we talked about your dog passing away.

DB: Yes. Well, that just made the wheels fall off the wagon for everything.

MF: So that happened in November, right? When did you do ketamine therapy?

DB: I just finished my first six-week series of it. So I started it probably in the middle of April [2024].

MF: What made you want to be part of it?

DB: Well, the talk therapy aspect is great. But I'm not a person who is terribly willing to put it out there. I'm very happy to take it from other people, but I'm not going to give it, right? And even with my delightful therapist, I could tell I was trying to give her mostly the good stuff, maybe a little bit of a song and dance.

MF: A little bit. Oh, yeah, I really can relate.

DB: I know you can. I just feel like some of the work you have to do is in-between your own ears. I had done some reading on it. And I thought, you know what, I'm just gonna do it, it can't hurt me. So I might as well just try it. I felt better just by taking that first action. Sometimes that first thing, just taking one step makes you feel better. That's why I told myself to give it a rip. I don't think I spent a lot of time thinking about it. It's interesting, because even while taking the medicine, I still have this weird third party in my head as this observer, rather than necessarily letting myself fully experience it. I don't know what that says about me. I signed up to do six more sessions because I feel like my brain is just starting to get the hang of this from a neuroplasticity standpoint. So I should probably do it a couple more times.

MF: When you tried ketamine, did you have certain outcomes in mind? What were some of the things that you wanted to accomplish?

DB: At first I had this laundry list of things, like objectives I was going to achieve. Then I realized that that probably wasn't exactly the right way to go into it, because that wasn't helping me to be part of the experience. In other words, my agenda was keeping me separate from the experience. So instead, I decided that I was really going to think about feeling like I've been walking around with a hole in my heart and I didn't expect that to just disappear, but maybe the edges of the hole would soften and the hole would get a little bit smaller. That was the visual I kept thinking about. Then any other expectation, whatever else happened, happened. And it's a weird thing because it's difficult to articulate.

My husband's like, "If A, then B, then all these things follow." But it wasn't linear like that for me.

Maybe that's happening neurochemically and you're not aware of it. It's almost like when you're in Marin County [outside of San Francisco] and the fog is in and then all of a sudden, little by little by little, you look and suddenly it's a bright blue sunny day. And, well, I don't know when that clarity actually happened for me.

I can't say I had some epiphany or an "Aha!" moment. I had felt so exhausted with the sale of the company, with the kid going to school and then with my sweet puppy dying. I was just sitting at the bottom of the well and the mud wasn't even wet anymore before I noticed where I was mentally.

All of my usual stuff that I could normally do was not there to help, so there was nothing filling up the well at all. I was just spent and I wouldn't say that my well is all the way full now, but somehow it's back at a good level. I don't know how it is, so I've decided that I don't need to. I can just be grateful for what is.

MF: You're a physician, so you did your research. I imagine you had enough data to know the possibilities and risk and all that stuff?

DB: I don't think anything really untoward can happen. I don't think that's a problem, but I will say that being a doctor in particular gives you this ability to detach, which is great because it makes you a good doctor, but that's not necessarily a good thing in many other settings. My husband was pulling info about it and he said, "Oh, here's this really cool paper on neuroplasticity," and I told him, "Dude, I don't want to read it. I liter-ally don't want to read it. I don't want to, I don't need to understand all the science. I want to just experience it." I would come out and say, "Okay, so tell me about it." But I couldn't yet, so I just sat there.

MF: I've tried some of the other stuff. I'm very much open to ketamine therapy, too. I'm trying to get off of antidepres-sants. I'm moving in that direction knowing there's all these other modalities to treat mental health issues. I've seen how many of them are effective.

DB: Oh, of course.

MF: I think of the possibilities, especially in plant medi-cine. You mentioned that you're going to continue doing this—does that mean you're still on this journey?

DB: Mindbloom is the company I use and they do these six sessions to start. For the first six, it's a little more prescriptive. You meet with the physician or a nurse practitioner or whatever. They send you the medication. It's all oral, so you really can't go wrong. You can only really get screwed up with ketamine if you're not doing it orally. You'd really have to try hard to mess it up, I guess, is what I'm saying. And then you have your coun-selor person that you work with.

They have a lot of groups that you can join online. I don't find that to be particularly helpful. That's just not my vibe. I'm like, this is all in-between my ears. I don't really need to talk about it with other people, but everyone's different. And it's guided, so you have the music and whatnot. They send you the whole kit and you take the medicine and check out for the next hour and a half; that is the program in a nutshell.

You do some journaling and then typically, you're kind of in La La Land for the rest of the day. I feel like the real magic happens on day four, five or six after the medicine wears off. That's where I think you're more open and there are new path-ways that are being created in your brain.

One of the things that really came up was that I felt this grief hole was closing. I don't think I'm going out on a limb here to say I am so much nicer to everyone else than I am to myself. Not, both in terms of my self-dialogue, but then also the grace that I'm willing to give other people.

MF: It's admitting to yourself, "*I'm* not okay."

DB: I haven't ever been in line for my own grace. I think that especially as I was nearing the end, the last couple sessions, that was one big insight for me. Not that it's shocking news to anyone, but that was definitely something that I was like, "Oh, okay, this is good to know." I think part of what we're talking about is that which makes you effective at your job, right? See, the ability to shut the fuck up and get on with it and all of these things that are all still there. That's going to be in my Round Two sessions. It sounds like there are plenty of folks who will do it once a week, six weeks, then they need to take a little break. I'm finishing up my break and then I'll do it again. I don't know if I'll do it once a week down the line. I might do it every other week. I'll wait and see, but then it seems that there's some good research along with what I hear anecdotally. I will likely do it once a month-ish or if I feel like I'm kind of getting stuck in a rut, just to open things up a little bit again. That's my plan.

MF: You mentioned something about how you are more forgiving of others than yourself. That's where I'm getting some clarity for myself. Does forgiveness factor into your grieving process? Like do you think the healing process in your sessions has extended to how you treat yourself?

DB: Yes, and I think every loss is also a gift. I had always sort of joked around like, "Oh, when Otis [my dog] dies, y'all are going to have to check me into the funny farm," and all this kind of stuff. Obviously knowing what all that was, neither having the time nor quite honestly, maybe the courage, to deal with it until you have no choice *but* to deal with it, you get what you get. I think that was definitely sweet little Otis's last gift to me. I got comfort and healing for that loss, which made me feel so much better internally.

MF: The other thing I thought about, too, is dealing with the trauma or grief of every unique exit. And especially in your case, it sounds like trauma for sure.

DB: Right. And for me, I couldn't help but wonder if that was the plan all along. Maybe I was too naive to see it? Was that the intention? Or was this really, "Oh, well, great opportunities come along. So let's ride with it." In all honesty, I still don't know. And that still sticks in my craw a little bit. Now I don't really give a shit as much.

MF: That's good. And in your involuntary exit, you mentioned that if you knew it was gonna be such a quick turnaround, you would have stayed at your previous position. What was that previous position and what was it giving to you that this wasn't?

DB: Well, I was running all the strategy and business development for a $1.5 billion company, which was really cool. It was a big physician partnership. I mean, they're the people who do work at Marin General and all over the place. There was an internal CEO search and it was between me and this other guy. The board picked the other guy. That was when I was going to start looking for something else. I had built out a great team. I was kind of, sounds horrible to say, but pretty easily done. I was making plenty of money and completely stuck in a rut. I had on these golden handcuffs. I probably could have put up with it and just done it, you know what I mean? So the reason I left was that I was ready to go for the new challenge. And then there would be a big payout at the end. That was enough activation energy to get me over the hump. If I'd known, oh, it's gonna be a pain in the ass and it's gonna be 10 months...

MF: And yeah, you're gonna get some money, but not a ton of money, ultimately.

DB: The decision analysis might have gone, "But who gives shit?"

My husband's like, "Who cares, man? You're so much happier having gone. Clearly, it was the right thing to do." Now

I can look back to see it and say it *was* the right thing to do. But in the middle of it, I did not have the ability to say that.

MF: It sounds like in the previous position, albeit with high certainty, it was like "eh," right? Now you're coming into maybe a higher upside, less certainty, which quickly became much less certainty. Aligning with your purpose has higher stakes because you yourself were entering into a higher growth mode.

DB: Yep, we're building towards something.

MF: Now you can create what you want.

DB: I think that's exactly right. Because I've sort of seen both sides. I'm from a risk and excitement profile to where I feel like I have a much broader appreciation. As a general rule, most physicians are not big risk-takers. It's a pretty risk-averse group of individuals. That said, I've always been very good at analyzing and then moving forward regardless, because you have to be a pretty good decision-maker in the moment. I was making plenty of money, but I was bored out of my mind. I guess that was fine until it wasn't. I am really glad that I did what I did and that I left because I learned a lot and it gave me a whole new set of skills. They were muscles that I knew I would have to exercise at some point, but I really wanted to flex them. I knew I was never going to have the opportunity to do so if I stayed where I was. It was kind of a selfish choice on my part. But I think it was a good choice. Now as I try to figure out what the eff I'm going to do next, I don't know, I have to see.

MF: Now you have this freedom.

DB: I don't have to go out and start something or join something right away.

MF: What's the most important next step for you?

DB: I don't mind working hard, but it's got to be something that I don't have to think about and we don't have to solve world peace. But it's got to be something that appeals to me and has some emotional resonance: work I love. I actually enjoy working hard. I've been very lazy since September, which is great, but I'm getting a little bored of that. When I look at all the things that I am actually doing—I'm doing a ton of stuff—I'm not laying around eating bonbons. At some point I'll be ready to be in a little bit more of a routine and I can feel that bubbling up already. I've been doing some consulting stuff, which is cool. I like chatting with people and mentoring and that kind of thing. It doesn't really pay the mortgage, but I feel like it's kind of giving back, so that's nice.

I can't really articulate it. I feel like if there was some turn-around thing where I thought, *Wow, that's kind of a cool concept, I would love to explore that.* I feel like that would be my ideal scenario.

My husband said, "Why don't you just go out and do it? Do what you were doing on your own because they bought it and they didn't do a very good job of it. And you would be great." But I feel like I already did that. I don't know if I want to redo taking charge. I suppose that's my ADD calling me. I'm kind of like, well, no, I've been there, done that. I don't need to do it again. I don't know. So, there it is.

MF: I completely get you. You kind of want to be busy, but busy doing the right thing.

DB: It's nice to have the privilege to be able to say "That's not the right thing. But *this* is."

MF: Oh, it's awesome. You've had these experiences and now you can build on those to see what comes next. I think our brains work in a similar way. I've had that instance before where I went through stages of grief around big work upheavals. I can see that it's automated in the way I react.

If I were one of your clients, how would you coach me if I came to you with something identical to what you just went through in terms of exiting?

DB: Well, I mean quite honestly, I think I would be like, "Hey, you should go read some Kübler-Ross [the clinician who developed the five stages of grief] and understand what grief is. Then recognize that grief and acknowledge it as grief. We can decide how you want to deal with that as best as we can." But I think even just giving your client the permission to recognize the event as a loss is powerful. It's almost like a little shameful secret. You're supposed to project, "Oh, isn't this great that I sold my company?" I almost feel like being able to help people name it as a loss and that you are in a grief process is a big deal. I feel like even just that has the clouds lifting a little bit. That would do for me.

MF: It reminds me of how I've felt with panic attacks. It's scary not knowing what's happening in your own body. But once you identify that, it's easier to see the severity of the feeling as immediately as if you're having a heart attack. I mean I've watched my heart rate climb to 180, 190 beats per minute. In my mind, it's gonna go to 240 and I'm gonna die because I can't even pick up the phone. Same kind of thing.

DB: It's all-consuming panic and grief in both the short and long term.

MF: There's this attitude that for anyone going through an exit, they should feel happy and grateful. The reality is, you grieve. That's a great message overall. I think that is a big, big thing for people to acknowledge.

DB: Yeah, I think that's it. Otherwise you have some shame around saying it to anyone.

MF: Exactly.

DB: Or even feeling it.

MF: Yeah.

DB: When you don't articulate those feelings to anyone, you end up internalizing all of it. That's when it comes out as a panic attack or whatever. It is fascinating to me. Last July, about a year ago, when we were right in the heart of all the due diligence stuff and I had done the denial phase, I had worked through it. Now I was just angry. I was never going to say that out loud, though. I wasn't going to sit in the room and say something, so I completely internalized it.

I had all these somatic things that started to happen. I threw my back out. All of the things that were happening to my body physically because I wasn't willing or able to voice that anger out loud. And I knew it. I couldn't even stand up. I couldn't go up the stairs. I saw the chiropractor and the acupuncturist. All of this stuff to "make me better," but none of that was going to make me better.

I just had to go underwater and scream, basically, which would have probably been the cheapest form of therapy available. Internalizing is what happens to the guys who end up with an ulcer because their body has to deal with those feelings one way or another. Your head's not going to take care of it, so the rest of you will. Then you get into this battle of what is mental health versus physical health? It's just wellness or a lack of wellness. The body and mind are not separate. But I think that's a big struggle for a lot of people to see when they are going through the process.

MF: Now that you have moved through the stages of grief, do you feel ready to find your purpose or to climb your second mountain? As exited entrepreneurs, we have to have a sense of purpose as a North Star to guide us.

DB: The short answer is yes. I want to point out first that exiting is a total change of identity, too. It's a lot of different losses packaged into one thing that is almost like it's your baby, your intellectual property, your identity. Because now all of a sudden, I'm the *former* [title] blah, blah, or, you know what I mean? That's also weird for people, I think.

MF: I know that grieving the exit as a loss is a big step, but finding a purpose is one way to move through that process. It's different for different people, right?

DB: Yeah, because the loss can mean different things to different people. I think it's one of those things where it would be so individualized based on all of the other things happening in someone's life, or even their previous experiences. I think even just being able to say it, where the commonality here is pretty clear. I think that's actually powerful, because I can imagine there are some people who, for them it's a loss and maybe they just made hundreds and hundreds of millions of dollars and they don't give a shit, they're just gonna go sit on an island. Although I don't think that people who make that kind of money are ever people who are willing to go sit on islands.

MF: It's true. I've talked to some of those people. I'm going to say a $100 million exiter, for example.

DB: Yeah, they're never going to run out of money.

MF: And it's like, "I'm going to do X, that's what I'm going to do. I'm going to go off and do X for however long."

DB: Right. Like run ultra marathons or whatever.

MF: A lot of them will say that they should buy a house on the beach and that will be it. There we go.

DB: Then it's all good.

MF: I mean, go do that.

DB: Right. But that won't satisfy you.

MF: The expectations of that satisfying you for the rest of your life will surely be met with disappointment.

DB: That's right. Achieving sustainable contentment has way more to do with finding your higher purpose and living authentically. I'm a firm believer that we need to continue to change and evolve, so long as we recognize what is temporary and what will last us forever. We can build skills and make money, but we will only be fulfilled if we're in alignment with our true selves, whoever that turns out to be.

RENEE METTY, PHD(C), M.ED

Renee Metty, PhD(c), M.Ed is the founder and CEO of With Pause, a Leadership Consultant and Equine Gestaltist and Facilitator.

Renee and I share the same business coach, Jeff Spencer. I remember being sort of nervous to meet new people at a 100-person mastermind, but I felt a small comfort knowing she'd be there, too. I made a beeline straight for her once the group had a few minutes to break. She immediately impressed me with her poise and ability to tap into her *ikigai*. She has substantial experience as an entrepreneur, namely as the founder of the first mindfulness-based preschool in the nation. She also owns a number of horses and has become invested in the benefits of Equine Gestalt Coaching (EGC). Her life as an entrepreneur is truly a lesson in *ikigai*.

Renee is the founder and CEO of With Pause, a training and development organization that offers consulting and private or group coaching to individuals or entrepreneurs. Renee has several entrepreneurial achievements that include running the successful event production company, It's Eventful. She is self-employed as an Equine Gestalt Coach and is continuing her studies to become a Master Gestaltist, following in the footsteps of her beloved mentor. Her foundational expertise rests with her experience as a special education teacher and as the founder of the early childhood school, The Cove School.

MARK FUJIWARA [MF]: What do you have going on these days?

RENEE METTY [RM]: I just got back from Denver. I went out to finish the fifth CORE intensive as part of the certification I needed. I had to be at five five-day stints in Colorado, plus three virtual four-day stints over two years to do my own personal work and to do some continued learning. I just came back on Sunday after an amazing experience. I have one more trip to go out there for more of a logistics and foundational intensive to finish.

MF: I love that because some of these coaching certifications online seem almost as if you can play them in the background, then take a test that you'll pass by 90 percent.

RM: Yes! So many programs can be completed so quickly. And by no means do I feel that being a certified coach necessarily makes you a great coach. I know plenty of coaches who are phenomenal with no official certification. That's why I became very aware of the fact that this is super special. There are slightly over 300 of us and under 100 of us who are dual grads becoming Master Gestaltists.

There are all these amazing people I've met in my Equine Gestalt Coaching program, founded by Melisa Pearce. She studied with Joseph Zinker, who contributed to the development and growth of Gestalt theory and methodology. Melisa and some of the original practitioners identified the need to move the Gestalt movement forward or contribute to it in perpetuity in some way. I knew I wanted to be a part of that, which is why I'm in training to be a Gestaltist.

It was two weeks ago I finished my last, what they called C-O-R-E intensives. This is the part of the program where we as practitioners do our own deep work and healing so we can sit with clients as presently and cleanly as possible. This helps differentiate the EGC program from therapists because therapists are not required to do their own work and healing. There are five COREs you attend in person. My fifth one was just last weekend. My fourth one happened to be, just because of the way the schedule fell, two weeks prior. I'm sitting at my fourth one going, "I'm not ready." I need like three more COREs. I need more. Do not launch me into the world in January. I went through this final one two weeks later where some people have six months in between them.

But that's when all the jigsaw puzzles started coming together and everything cemented in for me. I did all kinds of things, I practiced with clients, led open groups, set containers and things like that.

With this last intensive, I knew I was ready. It happens like that for a lot of us, almost all of us where we don't feel ready at first. I shared with the group by saying, "I am so humbled and honored to bring this work into the world to help people get through deep pain and suffering."

When you hear people's stories—and I know you've heard a lot of different things yourself—you just see humans are so resilient. I sometimes wonder, How are you a functioning human in the world? With the abuse and neglect, the addiction? As a parent, I am highly intentional and involved. But I sit there and I will always question, "As a parent, what am I doing or saying to my children that will cause them some pain or suffering in their adult life?" There is always something and we won't always know what it is.

Over two years, I had the opportunity to watch this woman come in like, "I should not be on the planet anymore," which was kind of her state of mind at the time. All to eventually become a confident coach, bright smiling and a completely different person. You can see that in an epigenetic piece where you pass generations, you pass it back and you remove it from epigenetic lines.

MF: I'm getting all this clarity about multiple situations from working through underlying causes in my addiction recovery. I realized that my precious energy was going everywhere. I have a coach named Jean Pierre LeBlanc who's done IFS with individuals and groups.

He said, "Just look at your triggers and then, you know, we could do it together."

But the more you do the inner work on yourself, the more you have confirmation of what you need to do externally. That's a little different than IFS work because it's more like internal alchemy. It removes a lot of the IFS work that's normally done for a typical person. Recently our group prac-

ticing IFS talked through what it means to be "stalled." One person in particular got specific, and he goes, "Oh, wow. It started way back with my mom." All of a sudden he's able to see those emotions stemming from being abandoned by his mom. He was on the brink of divorcing his wife. Then he has this conversation with her where after he says, "I was able to identify it wasn't you that was triggering me. Because I showed up this way, surprising her by acknowledging I was projecting."

RM: So it's about dealing with life right now in this moment and it doesn't always mean we blame our parents or the experiences we had in childhood.

It seems like at least half the people I've interacted with lately are dealing with narcissistic mothers where they have to peel away at how and why they've created these blocks—why they created this skewed viewpoint of themselves. I'm fascinated with narcissism. Fascinated! I just found out that narcissism typically happens because of an injury in infancy. Somewhere between birth and 18 months old, there's an injury. You're not born with it.

MF: Amazing.

RM: As you were talking about what is essentially group therapy, I was thinking about Equine Gestalt Groups. The biggest difference between the two is that group therapy tends to be a "talk about" session that offers tools and strategies, whereas Gestalt Groups offer people an experience and more often than not remove the charge/trigger from our systems completely. It's one of so many beautiful things we can do to take care of ourselves.

MF: I recently discovered the power of self-care through Japanese calligraphy.

When I was at my lowest point, [my wife] Amy said, "You've got to figure something out to really care for yourself." So learning how to care for yourself is the key.

RM: Yes, and as high achievers it can't be like you run yourself into the ground. What tends to happen as high achievers begin to care for themselves or get on this path, is they turn self-care or practicing presence as another thing to achieve, which runs me into the ground all over again.

I'm in the process of creating coursework and it just keeps getting deeper and deeper as I think about raising my own children. I am not as interested in teaching about discipline, potty training and kind of that surface-level stuff. I will, but I am much more passionate about how we raise conscious humans and what the ecosystem of repairing and healing the past is so that you can be as present as possible to create the future that you want for your kiddos. What's the foundation for your children to be able to be the best humans that they can be? And I keep going back and forth, but I need to trust that it's in the hands of the right people.

MF: Yes, because you want to make sure that they will understand it.

RM: Yes, absolutely! Everything, all my leadership coaching, training and development overlaps with parenting in some way. We are in the space of human development and human consciousness. If anybody has children, they usually realize that showing up differently at home and work doesn't feel great. We are modeling for our children, especially in this day and age of remote work. Children pay attention and absorb more of what you do and less of what you say or tell them. How do I show up best for my children? At some point, when we're founders, when we're owners of businesses, when we're high achievers with a high purpose, it can be hard for the family unit to understand why our focus is out here for the greater good. How do we balance that to make sure that our family unit, which is incredibly important to us and the whole picture, either feels like they're part of it or understands? Because that can create a real divide.

You're out here helping millions of people, thousands of people, hundreds of people and you're so passionate, but what do our immediate family members get? The rest of us—they get the rest of us. And how do we reconcile that?

MF: I told Amy and she agreed. I said, "I'm so sorry, I've been giving my energy to everybody else but you and [our daughter] Stella." Sometimes she would come down here to my office and she would hear me on a call.

She would say, "Wow, I don't ever see that side of you, you know."

RM: Yes, it's wild isn't it? Maybe if they saw more of that then they would understand. I don't know, it's different for everyone. Then there's a whole bunch of stuff wrapped into that in terms of our worth and identity, too. Especially for moms. We either go right back to work or I know I spent a decade raising children and squeezing in work. I think I told you I was doing all this great work in the world when I thought, *We need to get divorced.* I'm a mom, but now I found work that I love and why do I have to choose? And how do I separate the two? Then I separated too much and there's a lot in that decision to make things whole. That's the delicate ecosystem. Thankfully I realized pretty quickly that it wasn't that I wanted to give up on my marriage or being a mom, I just didn't want to have to cook, clean and all the things. I absolutely loved being a part of a family unit and raising our children. I was able to reclaim myself and what I love while being a mom and wife. Children must see that process too.

Now the people we often work with, entrepreneurs and founders have partners/spouses who need the support because when someone is doing personal growth work, the person on the personal growth track, without really realizing it or doing it consciously, is creating a separation somehow. By changing internally, you're changing the contract with the people around you and how you once related to them. It is so important to keep your partner in the loop and potentially renegotiate the contract with their input.

We get this energetic high almost from doing the deep

growth work, then we start speaking the same language of the heart to other people in our lives. It doesn't mean they have to be on the same path as you. My husband and I were meeting in the middle and then apart and then meeting in the middle and now he's starting to trust his intuition more to meet me where I am. It has been an incredible journey honoring each other on this path.

MF: I used to project onto Amy that she didn't want me to do these big things at work because she didn't want me to succeed. She felt like, because in the past when I did travel, it would take me away from her and Stella.

I think it really hurt me deeply when she said, "Oh, she doesn't want her own dad to get her upstairs when she's awake in the morning. She doesn't want her dad when she falls asleep at night."

RM: I think that's super important to see, too. The healing is going to be amazing. It takes work with both people in the relationship to see when our defenses kick in and what we communicate to each other at that moment. With children, it is in the timing, especially when they are young'; it is all about who is present with them the most. It is hard for dads, too, when you are the primary source of income or even holding the perspective that the man provides for the family. That is a somewhat primal and deeply ingrained perspective. These are important conversations to have with our partners.

MF: Not every person we encounter is very conscious of their purpose or *ikigai* and striving for that. See, what you're doing, and what I'm trying to do, is something that says to me, "You're breaking away from the norm because you're finding the highest level of purpose possible." I want to help other exited entrepreneurs find their higher purpose.

RM: Ah yes!! The work you are doing is so important. So many founders have their identity wrapped up in what they've created. It can be a harsh reality when you exit your company. There is definitely a transition and integration period. For me, it all comes back to trust: trusting that you are exactly where you need to be in that moment. Building trust with myself was a big part of my journey. We did a lot of exercises on Sunday playing with people's intuition, which is to trust if you're connected to God, source, the universe or whatever connection you have that is larger and outside of yourself.

Just like honing your mental game or physical strength, you can hone your intuition and trust. We did a bunch of exercises to help eliminate skepticism. Not everyone in the program is quick to embrace this phenomenon of intuition. So we played with dowsing rods and a pendulum to experience energy, and then we played with our intuitive abilities. We all have them, but some people are more open and trust themselves more than others.

Our trainer had us all sitting in a circle facing out, where some of us held up a piece of paper the trainer had written on earlier in the session. So, a stop sign was written on a person's piece of paper and she says, "Okay, hold the image in your mind, this is something you've all seen," and she adds, "Hold that image in your mind's eye and ask the rest of us about its color, shape, purpose." We all had to call out our guesses and I can't tell you how many times some image flashed so quickly and my brain got in the way. I should have said the first thing that came to mind, but I often second-guessed myself. Then I tuned it up and I got on a roll. I was starting to discern the difference between when it was my mind versus the quick feeling associated with the image. It is a helpful exercise to begin discerning your ego from the essence.

It might be fuzzy, but the feeling is accurate. I come from the school of thought that the body never lies. These exercises were really about trusting yourself. You don't have to learn something new. It's already in all of the people that you're going to be meeting with. It's in you, too.

We are already equipped with everything we need. We just have to peel away the layers so we get the clarity to see it, feel it and know it.

JENNIFER K. HILL

Jennifer K. Hill is the CEO & co-founder of OptiMatch and keynote speaker/executive coach. She built and exited a profitable company and is a member of Deepak Chopra's Evolutionary Leaders Group.

During one memorable group session, my business coach invited four of his top entrepreneurs to connect. Jennifer was one of those individuals, and I'm extremely grateful to have met her. Mental health has always been a huge priority for her. She has this great ability to balance the heaviness of some of her struggles with the lightheartedness of being a truly free spirit.

Jennifer has the unique ability to engage with her Higher Power when it comes to issues at work. She is authentic and kind, warm and insightful. Jennifer and I began our friendship swiftly because we disclosed everything about our mental health issues upfront. It was off to the races from there.

When I shared with Jennifer that I was tapering off of my antidepressants, her immediate response was, "Let me be your support system." She is open about her struggles, which disarms others and gives them the space to share just as much about themselves with her. Unsurprisingly, Jennifer attracts other wonderful and authentic entrepreneurs like Melissa Bernstein [whose interview is featured later in this book]. Jennifer agreed to introduce me to Melissa, though with the caveat that it might take a while for me to hear back from her.

That same afternoon I reached out, and Melissa emailed me back to say, "I cannot wait to meet you."

Friendships like what I've developed with Jennifer continue to lead to other fulfilling relationships in my personal and professional life.

JENNIFER K. HILL [JH]: It's such a pleasure to connect with you, Mark. I'm so grateful for that. I wanted to learn more about your story and what lights you up as a human being to see if I could support you in any way.

MARK FUJIWARA [MF]: I can't tell you how happy I am to be talking with you about mental health as an exited entrepreneur. I recently helped a friend of mine who was feeling suicidal, and the only way I knew how to do that was by speaking from the heart and simply being there for her. I made sure she knew, "Hey, I've been there, too."

JH: I'm like you, Mark. The first time I tried to take my own life, it was with a bunch of aspirin and wine coolers. This happened when I was 18 years old. On one of the next two of my attempts, I took an entire bottle of sleeping pills. Suddenly, I came to, and my car was hanging off the side of a cliff. Just by sheer happenstance, somebody found me. I was just losing it. I thought, *How am I supposed to kill* me? I was only 20 years old, happy to be driving down this remote road where my car was off-cliff where I was found.

At one point, I went down to Mexico and got tons of Valium, but I couldn't tell you how many I took. I probably took, I don't know, 40 or 50 pills, and somehow another one of my roommates found me and saved me. People took care of me and I would say the only thing that stops me when I have really, really, really, really hard dark days of the soul, where I just want to crawl up in a ball and die, is the Kabbalah [a popular form of Jewish mysticism]. The Kabbalists say that if we take our own lives, we have to come back and we have to do it all over again, but it's harder the next time. That is the only thing that keeps my feet planted on Earth. Because there are many days—and I've had two of them in the last three weeks—where I've just been curled up in a ball. When I'm depressed, I'm like, okay, I know what I need to do. I need to meditate, I need to do acts of kindness for other people.

One day I was so crushed, I was trying to work out at a Pilates studio and I was curling up in a ball, crying, sobbing on the Pilates studio floor, like three weeks ago.

I decided to record messages for others. I recorded myself in between sobs. It was me just trying to lift myself out of it, but also to help other people. I was like, "Dear entrepreneur, I know sometimes you just want to call it quits, you are so enraged and so angry that you feel like you're not going to survive this." And, "Dear entrepreneur, I know that this is scary and that you feel like nobody will ever understand…."

I wound up sharing it with my husband and three or four entrepreneurs and every one of them, whether or not they've ever experienced suicidal thoughts, said, "I needed that because people just don't get it." No matter where they were as entrepreneurs.

Somebody else said, "You might want to change that to 'human,'" because things go wonky sometimes and I don't know about you, but the times where I've tried to kill myself or wanted it to end it all were times I felt like I couldn't be fully human. I remember the last time I felt it very, very clearly when I was truly suicidal. This was years ago when my husband and I were in Paris and we got in a fight over something stupid. Because I'm neurodiverse, I sometimes struggle to communicate. My ex-husband complained about this as well. I'll try to solve a problem rather than ask, "Oh, how are you feeling?" At the time, I said I was never going to be able to give that to somebody. I have been doing 20 years of personal development work and I just suck at being human. Thank God I have a very supportive husband where if I am suicidal or anything I just tell him and then we have beautiful conversations. He holds space for it, but it sucks sometimes.

Thank you for being an amazing friend, if you haven't heard that lately. Thank you for being there for somebody in their dark time.

MF: No, thank you for sharing all that. I can completely relate. I sense that we are similar in that we are both very, very sensitive, especially in terms of energy and emotion. I can be dragged down easily and it will spiral so quickly. Little things can make me spiral and I think that's a big challenge of entrepreneurship because we don't ever have certainty.

I also feel that sometimes in bad times, we go down that familiar road and things can get very dark very quickly. But I think it happens even in good times, too, because I tend to feel a little bit more lonely in those times. That's what some of these exited entrepreneurs are sharing with others in groups—that they feel isolated because when you're doing so well, or you have a ton of money in the bank, there's this idea that you shouldn't be having these negative thoughts.

JH: I know. I fight about this with one of my best friends I've had for 20 years, though I lovingly call her my platonic soulmate. I'll complain to her, saying, "Listen, I have an amazing life. I have a husband I love and a wonderful life. I get to help people, I get to travel the world."

On paper, most people say, "You have a dream life." So I feel as if it's unfair for me to ever complain about anything.

My best platonic soulmate friend will tell me to snap out of it by saying, "You're allowed to have feelings, you're allowed to have a tough day and just because you have a life that looks good on paper does not mean that you don't get to cry or have hard days or say it sucks sometimes." I think that speaks to your point.

This all keeps things in perspective. That's why I try to do things to keep the perspective that if something small happens, I'm allowed to feel sad or upset. But at the same time, am I going to survive it? Yes, and it's about getting ourselves out of our familiar loop. Even if you have it all, you still go through it.

MF: I've started to see that exited entrepreneurs are a very misunderstood group. I think there are just so many misconceptions out there about how success feels, versus the reality. Every single exited entrepreneur I've spoken to has had some form of mental health struggle, but most do not have the tools to cope.

That is why I'm convinced that getting these folks together can be extremely powerful. We can help each other figure these things out. When I do things like breath work by myself, it's

amazing. **But when I do breath work with people I love and respect, it opens up a whole new level of clarity.**

JH: I love that breathwork and all of that. That's so powerful. I use the Heart-Focused Breathing (HFB) technique daily. I got to know the practice about four years ago and there's something that all of a sudden I discovered I can do, going back to talking to your dead relatives. I learned a thing called soul talking that one of my colleagues, a holistic teacher, has called "proactive confrontation." Let's say you have to have a challenging talk with your wife, your daughter or your business partner. You first ask yourself at the soul level, "Is this person available to have this conversation?" Asking that would solve 99 percent of the world's problems.

Four or five years ago, when my teacher started teaching me this work, I would ask your soul, "Mark, are you available to have conversations all of a sudden?"

People's souls started telling me more than just "yes" and "no."

Then I'd ask more specific questions like, "Is this really about your sister who's having mental health struggles?"

Then the person would respond, "How do you know that?"

I'd answer with, "Your soul just told me." I never thought I'd be in a place to teach this to people.

My dad was in the hospital and passed away in February [2024]. It was a crazy thing because in early January, I was on a call with him and I just knew he was going to die 30 days later. When he was in the hospital, it was completely unexpected to everyone else. It wasn't like he had cancer or anything like that. While my dad was in surgery before he passed away, I was talking to dad's soul and my mom asked, "Can you teach me to do that?"

I didn't know—*can* I teach you? I asked the Source and the Source said, "Yes, you can."

MF: I'm so sorry to hear about your loss, Jennifer.

JH: Thank you. What's crazy is, I realized that Heart-Focused

Breathing work allows us all to connect to anybody at the living or the deceased soul level.

I'm getting a new HeartMath [HeartMath incorporates biofeedback technology, breathing techniques, meditation and mindfulness practices and emphasizes the importance of emotional intelligence and developing healthy coping mechanisms] done, so I want to tell you a couple of things with that.

What's interesting about HeartMath, too, is that a lot of what I do now, especially, is to determine a person's character, if they're authentic or not. I've met other people who do that, who see if you're in a natural state of coherence with the other person. If coherence is down, if they're talking about something traumatic or something like that, obviously your coherence might be down, too. But as I record the conversation, you can go back and you can see at the eight-minute mark, "Whoa, it dropped."

MF: Wow.

One of my oldest friends and I met in 2008 so randomly at one of Jenny McCarthy's masquerade balls. She had a psychic there who wound up becoming my business mentor. She told me about the guy who would eventually change my life. She said, "Jen, there's gonna be a male that you're gonna hire and he's gonna change your life." This guy came into my office one day, his name is Mark. It was maybe three or four years into my last company and people were not sold on him being the right person. He was very sweet, if not a bit awkward, unemployed, but I knew I liked him.

I thought he was perfect and everybody else was asking, "Are you sure he is the one?"

I insisted, "He is *it*." I just energetically felt it the moment I met him. I'm so happy to say he just left the company. It was maybe a couple of months ago, which was his 10th anniversary at the company.

When I first saw him, I felt that connectedness immediately. I will recoil from people's energy sometimes. I can read photos of

people. I can look at photos of animals or people. I can sometimes tell when people are going to die. It can be very scary.

I don't like to mess with that, though. My friend once sent me
a picture of this little girl on an email with people bcc'd and she
said, "Please pray and meditate for this little girl." I didn't know
who she was. The moment I saw her photo, I knew she was
going to die 24 hours later. So I told my husband. Sure enough,
the little girl died 24 hours later.

Same thing with my dad. This has been happening more and
more. I can read good or bad energy, but I will tell you my little
secret: I say the "anti-jerk" prayer every day to protect myself. I
came up with this three years ago. I find it works so well because
I throw it all out to the universe. My husband knows I would
give my life for him. I love him with all my heart and soul. Every
day I say out loud, "Universe, remove anything or anyone who
is not in my highest good. Give me the wisdom to know what's
happening for my God and through God, the right people and
resources towards me."

**MF: I think you have a sophisticated way of vetting the
people in your life.**

JH: I told my friend, Jewels, about your "plus two" paradigm
[otherwise known as the abstraction principle, where the
purpose is to transform a low-level situation into a higher-level
one]. We share tools that we pick up with each other.

She said, "Jen, you've taught me a lot of great stuff lately. But
I want to let you know that the one tool that has unequivocally
changed my life in the last three weeks is the plus two."

You've changed one of my best friend's lives, so thank you
for that.

**MF: It's so powerful. I think the plus two thing has evolved
for me. It started like this: I would see that a person is plus two
—the relationship is worth it to me because they are bringing
more to the table than they are taking. But then I start to see
this subconscious thing happen where I'm exerting more
energy than I'm getting back into the relationship. Once I see**

someone move from the plus two deal, I'll disconnect. I've had to do that with clients.

JH: One of the things I do business deal-wise whenever my husband has a big business deal he's about to invest in, we say to the universe, "If it's in my highest and best good, and humanity's highest and best good for this deal to happen, then please let it happen with ease. If not, please lovingly redirect us all to the right partners and send prosperity to everybody in the deal ."

It's complete surrender. It's not always perfect.

Have you worked on developing your intuition and talking out loud to your higher self every day? Have you tried that? I do talk out loud and it's actually to my mentor who passed away last year.

MF: Oh, amazing. Yeah, me too. My mentor was Larry Heyward [creator of the plus-two paradigm shift and former Chairman and CEO of Leslie's Poolmart, Inc.]. It was because of breathwork that I truly connected with him.

He asked me, "Why aren't you talking to me?" So one day I just started talking to him.

I'd say, "Hey, this thing is going off the rails," and I would have a dialogue with Larry.

But you're also speaking about talking to your higher self or whatever you call Source.

JH: Something that one of my other teachers taught me a couple of years ago is to talk out loud to whatever Source or higher self you can, call it whatever you want, whatever your contact is. What I do is every morning after I do my meditation, I immediately go into Heart-Focused Breathing, then I do inner child work and then I talk out loud to what I consider Source or self. I say the sets of prayers I've mentioned. I go through a series of questions that are "yes" and "no" that sometimes go more in-depth.

I ask every day what my purpose is by asking specifically, "Today, how can I serve the greater good?" As you develop this, you'll notice you become a clear audience, which is honing your ability to hear, just as you're hearing with your mentor. Then I cross-check how accurate my intuition is. For a while in 2020, when my husband was in crypto—I'm not really in that space—I bought some just for fun and I didn't know what to ask for, so I asked if today was a good day to buy myself crypto.

I hear, "Yes, buy."

Somebody told me I should have listened to this at the time, but I could hear Source say, "Sell" very clearly and "Don't buy." It was a great year, though.

MF: This is going to be a huge part of what we talk about here with things that are helpful for exited entrepreneurs. You've mentioned some amazing practices in terms of what I love about the true self, authenticity and focusing on your heart center—all the wonderful spiritual skills you have. It's powerful that you can predict things, like in the case of the child. But I feel like if a lot of these entrepreneurs can tap into something like that, it would become a big part of their healing.

Thank you for being so vulnerable, I appreciate that, too.

JH: Thank you, Mark. I love that you shared your heart. I've been through addiction and hard times myself. I did crystal meth every day for six months when I was younger. I've been through my share of hard times and addiction, so anything I can do to help you as you go through this process.

MF: Just by hearing that, that healed me a lot. I appreciate that. I also want you to know, I get where you're coming from, as well. I completely understand and am honored that you shared all that with me—I will not take that lightly. If you're in a situation where you're just like, "I don't know how I feel," reach out to me because it lifts me up to help. It doesn't lift me that I know you're hurting, but it lifts me that I can be of service to you one hundred percent. I've watched friends who have gone through it and come out the other side and I always tell them if you want to get help I will help you through.

JH: My sister was homeless for a month several years ago.

She started self-medicating instead of her bipolar meds and she had a schizophrenic break. It was crazy and it was the hardest thing to see. You know how they say vampires turn off their emotions? That's how that period was with my family because my sister was unwilling to get help at first and I just held space for her while holding the firmest boundary.

I was the one in my family—despite having a mom and a dad who supported me through awful times—I told them, "Listen, if she's going to get healthy, here's how it's going to look. We're going to hold a firm boundary with her. We're not going to let her live with us, but we're going to do everything we can to help her."

She was homeless for a month and that crushed our whole family. But one day she called when she got to the hospital and she said, "Jenny, I need help. I need help. I know that there's something wrong." It was funny at the time when she told me, "I know that I think I'm Mother Mary incarnated and that you're part of a secret club called the Love Club that's here to save humanity." It sounded like every subsequent project I got involved with felt predetermined by this thing she said seven years ago.

I mention all that, Mark, to say that it's now seven years later and she is sober. She is healthy. She had a second son. I have a great relationship with her and my family. We all go through the dark night of the soul and the more we can, we need to hold space for somebody else going through theirs.

I think you would like my friend who passed away—Dr. Mark Goulston—for if you are ever having a hard time and you can't reach somebody, or if you have a friend like your friend earlier who needs wisdom. Mark passed away on December 31st of this last year, and he was one of the only psychiatrists ever who was a suicide expert to never lose a single patient to suicide.

He saved my life when I was going through suicidal ideation during my divorce and getting diagnosed as being autistic in 2018. When he passed away, it was like a punch in the gut. Then

I remembered Mark and I are connected on a soul level. So I just said, "Mark, it's me again." It's like he's still my friend.

He said, "Life is great over here. Remember how I could only mentor so many people at the physical level?"

Now anytime I meet somebody who is dealing with suicide themselves or has friends dealing with it, I tell them to call on Mark's soul. He did this beautiful series in the last few months of his life called "I'm Dying to Tell You" that was on *YouTube*, which was prolific. He wrote the best book in the world on listening called *Just Listen*. He is one of the most empathetic souls ever and he is wildly available to people.

He even just popped in right now and he said, "Yeah, Jen, I'm here."

We all need that kind of connection.

MELISSA BERNSTEIN

Melissa Bernstein is the co-founder of Melissa & Doug Toys, the co-founder of Lifelines, LLC and has exited two multimillion-dollar businesses.

I am fully convinced that meeting Melissa was made possible by divine intervention. As I said, my friend and fellow entrepreneur Jennifer K. Hill [whose interview you just read] introduced me to Melissa because she knew we'd have a wealth of topics to talk about. She was right, of course—Melissa and I bonded instantaneously over mental health issues, being exited entrepreneurs and the challenges and triumphs of living life seeking higher purpose. Melissa is the co-founder of the beloved toy company Melissa & Doug Toys, a business she and her husband exited after 36 years. Lifelines is Melissa's current business venture, where she leads the company to create products that ease stress through sensory immersion.

MARK FUJIWARA [MF]: I'm honored to speak with you, not only about your companies, but because I've admired you from afar. Everything that Jennifer says about you, too—I feel like there's a lot of these similarities in terms of our vulnerabilities as exited entrepreneurs.

MELISSA BERNSTEIN [MB]: I'm so curious. Tell me where you are and these vulnerabilities that we don't share enough of.

MF: You're right, we don't share enough. Mental health issues stem from my mom's side of the family, on the Chinese side. If I started feeling sad or even sick, I would tell my mom and she would say, "That can't happen," because even sickness is perceived as a weakness to a parent in this culture. My dad's Japanese; there was much more of a stoicism from his side of the family.

MB: You were broken and didn't know. The Japanese side's all about honor and the eightfold thing [this refers to the "eight-fold fence" from an ancient Japanese poem that features the deity Susanoo-no-Mikoto who built eight layers of fences (or "manyfold" fences) to protect his wife, symbolizing protection from threats].

MF: My dad used to walk around with gout. Looking back, I would never have known he was in pain or discomfort. That's because showing weakness, especially on the Japanese side, is unacceptable. My parents would say, "There's no reason why you have to be depressed. And the panic attacks! Oh my goodness, why are you so anxious? You have no kids and you're not married. Making more money than you spend, huh?"

Then I had a close cousin in our family take his own life. My dad showed me kindness and comfort when he said, "I want you to do two things for me. One, I want you to grieve every single day for the rest of your life if you need to, but never ever blame yourself for this. The second thing is, this is a test of character and strength. You're going through the hardest time of your life right now. Sometime in the future—it won't happen tomorrow—but sometime in the future, just think about how you can take this and make it into something good."

That's why I am insistent on offering a small group of exited entrepreneurs my number on speed-dial. I need them to know we are able to lean on each other in our time of need, no matter what the circumstances.

MB: Yeah, I love that. I can resonate. I have a small group of women who also exited their companies and we do our own group together.

Doug and I exited our company this year and I'd say the process of extricating was no less than a death. It was like watching my child be dismembered in front of me and not being able to do anything about it. It was one of the most heart-wrenching and grueling processes that I've ever experienced, because it cut to the core of meaning for me.

I think when we start these entrepreneurial ventures from deep within our essence, they are embedded in our DNA and our central nervous systems. They're part of who we are. We sort of think when they go, we'll just do something else. And that's what I thought. I thought, *I don't have an ego. My ego's not in this. I'll just go and sprinkle fairy dust on something else.* And then you realize it's not that easy.

So I get that. And I've spoken to so many women who've done the same thing and just crash because suddenly their conduit to meaning is basically turned off.

And here's the crazy thing: we sold for a billion dollars. Everybody was saying "Congratulations!" to me, because it was all about the dollar amount, right? A billion dollars and I couldn't get to that level of excitement even if I wanted to.

I texted my son, "I am like the lowest I've ever been in my life." No one is even thinking that it might not be a moment for celebration, but that's because they're latching on to the quantitative.

They say, "You did it!" And I'm like, no, I let my company down. I didn't do what I should have done. We made a mistake. All the things that I was second-guessing were all I was thinking about at the time.

My friend, Sara, was telling me, "I don't know what I'm gonna do next," and we were sobbing together about our exits. We were at a women's retreat and it was all of the folks who thought they were doing something good by giving up control, but all of us ended up feeling like we abandoned our souls in the process.

MF: Well, Melissa, it's bad enough to sell your company that you've built, right? It's tough enough emotionally, I should say, to sell your company. But when you do it with private equity, that's a different story altogether.

MB: Well, Doug and I both got ousted. So our story is crazy. We did it three times. We waited 20 years, like we owned 100 percent for 20 years. So we had the joy of what it was to do it completely on our own. The stakes kept getting higher. And that's what ultimately happens. The Piper—or the Reaper in our case—comes calling. We were still growing. We're probably the only toy company still growing. But it wasn't enough growth for the private equity firm. I never thought that I would get ousted. I was the creative mind; I was the idea person. I realized that they wanted the textbook way and they hired Kinsey [Kinsey Capital Partners, a Chicago-based private equity firm] to do their little thing—how they suck every ounce of value out of the company. Like every good thing we ever did. That's what ended up happening. I never got to say goodbye to my team after 32 years together.

It was so traumatic that I'm really not even supposed to share. I was supposed to keep it quiet, but now that we're sold, it's whatever. It was bad. But I will say that I have come to the other side through a lot of work. I can say now that it freed me from a prison and the anxiety I feel these days can be the dizziness of freedom. So when that freedom hits you and you don't know what you're freed for, you'll go into an existential vacuum and you will want to end your life. But if you can find your way through that abyss of nothingness and find other things to sink your teeth into, it will be a gift.

I had to stare the abyss of terror in the face and say, "Am I truly a white space creative? Or am I about being in a very comfortable, safe place where I can feel good about ideas and a team makes them? Or am I what I say I am and can I go back to the blank canvas and start again?"

I was terrified beyond belief that I couldn't do it again and that my life of creativity was over. But then I said, "You know what, I am going to try again. And I might fail and I might not, but I have to, I owe it to myself to try."

So my husband and I did it again. And now we are in that awful space of a startup, but we are doing what we are meant to do and what we love. I think that's the only way I began to feel okay again, to continue to channel darkness into light and make meaning and just take ideas and bring them to life and hopefully stay untethered to the result a little less than we were before. That's all that any of us can continue to do.

Find another beautiful method of impacting humanity.

MF: And it really is beautiful what you're doing.

MB: Well, that's all I can do. I was born with an existential meaning crisis, from my first breath, I was like, "Why am I here? What's the point of this absurdity? And what am I supposed to do with my time here?" If I'm not continually channeling that chaos into tangible form and some sort of meaning that can impact others, I go down really quickly and I could easily see me standing on a rooftop somewhere.

My wise existential psychotherapist says to me, "Doing is your form of being, and creating is your form of being." So I can't just sit idly there because then the rumination starts. I have to continue doing, connecting to creation that connects me to humanity and makes me feel that I have a point in being here.

MF: Do you get the sense that traditional psychiatric medicine or alternative therapeutic modalities helped you in a significant way as you were going through your traumatic exit?

MB: Generally speaking, I have a natural skepticism about pharmaceuticals in general. Do you realize people get you on it in 15 minutes? And then no one ever talks about "how" and "if" and "when" you're getting off of them. It's like an automated response when we are trying to get well.

MF: It's great for the pharmaceutical companies. For eight years, Melissa, I went to the psychotherapists and their questions were there simply to make sure that I kept on my meds. They do the opposite of what they're supposed to do. I know that trauma happens. I went through a nasty divorce and I'm still experiencing PTSD from it. But then the response is always, "Let's up the dose." I've started to realize that anxiety is the most human feeling and anxiety can be a precursor to growth.

MB: Exactly. If you are unable to feel anxious, you can't grow and evolve. Exactly.

MF: Yes. so I went to my primary care provider and I said, "Find me somebody who is more of a functional physician." Now I have two doctors, one on the other side of it, just having options with modalities that aren't attached to prescription meds.

And the psychiatrist is saying, "Okay, we've got to taper you off of these meds ASAP, we've got to do this." It makes a huge difference to work with a team of medical professionals to help me get to the core of my mental health issues, rather than staying dependent on meds.

MB: I never allowed myself to go on medication because I was so terrified about what it would do to me. I've had to navigate this horrible existential anxiety on my own.

My husband was having terrible anxiety at one point, maybe 10 years ago. He went to this psychiatrist that his primary care physician recommended and they put him on Klonopin. By the way, you're only supposed to be on Klonopin for a short time. He was on it for months and then started to become, like, waxed —he's the most positive person ever, but that changed during that time.

Then he started to go off the medicine cold turkey because no one told him about the negative effects to expect. And that's when he literally was going to jump off a building, so he had to end up getting a doctor to do the tapering thing to help him.

But this guy put him on it, a guy who's been a psychiatrist who never said a word about when to get off of the meds or how. I mean, that's how awful the psychiatric community is these days.

MF: Yeah, I went to my doctor and the same thing happened. My physician, who's a really good friend of mine, just said, "Hey, you need to go to this person to get help." She put me on Escitalopram [an antidepressant categorized as a selective serotonin reuptake inhibitor (SSRI)].

I said, "For how long?"

And she goes, "You're kind of going through a tough space, so we will see."

I was suicidal. I had planned out my suicide. I almost jumped off the Golden Gate Bridge a week before that. But she kept me on it because she saw I was feeling good, even though I'd had this very recent traumatic experience that I clearly hadn't yet worked through.

MB: And then it's about liability, right? Everyone's covering their asses. It's like you're feeling okay, just don't change a thing.

MF: Right. I mean the first five minutes of every appointment were like, "How are you feeling?"

"I'm feeling good."

Then, "Okay. So it's working for you, right?"

"Yeah, it's working for me."

"Okay, keep going. Any trauma?"

I didn't have any trauma I was gonna tell her about. If I had said "Yes, I have trauma," then she'd say, "Let's increase it, increase it, increase it."

MB: Well, people say to me, because everyone in my life who is on them [antidepressants], they say, "I can't cry." When you're on these, you get to the dose that has you not being able to actually feel emotions. And I mean, to think that you can't feel emotions is scary to me. If you're at a suicidal place, I always say, your baseline is zero and you're at negative 10. You need that to get you to zero so you can even begin to start doing the work. You're not going to do the work when you're not able to get out of bed. That's where I think we lack information. We don't have that halfway house that's just for regular anxiety that is actually pretty common to all of us these days.

MF: No, that's true. Everyone has anxiety to varying degrees.

MB: Yeah, I think that might be my defiant act of the human spirit, to *not* end my life. I always say both the beauty and the pain of the world are unbearable to me, because I am a feeler.

When it's too beautiful, I can't bear it. It's a beauty that is inde-scribably painful. And when it's dark, it's indescribably horrific.

MF: I had one of those dark moments yesterday, so I went to a 12-step meeting. Somebody shared something with me that got me to see where I was headed on my path. I knew that if I didn't get help at the right time, it would be really bad for me.

MB: I studied existential analysis and logotherapy, which is healing through meaning. Then I came across this woman, Emmy Van Deurzen; I read 10 of her books. Because what I think you also have, it's not a pathological illness–it's a spiritual soul crisis. It's a meaning crisis, because no one understands it. It's pathologized and we're given medication. If you believe that all humans have a will to meaning and if you do not find your meaning, by definition, you will fall into an existential void.

From a young age, I've been very connected to my soul and my purpose. So when I felt I didn't have one, I wanted to end my life. But when I feel that I am engaging in the steps to making meaning, I'm okay.

I feel like I belong here and I matter and there's something to do in my time here. So I wrote to this woman who wrote the 10 books that changed my life and I said, "Would you consider speaking with me?" She's a professor, a dual PhD and she founded the School of Existential Psychotherapy in Europe. She agreed and she's been my therapist for four years now, which has changed my life. She's the only one who truly understands what I go through. So at a very low point, like about a year ago, I felt like a rainbow that had lost all its colors. When I go low, I feel like the darkness is taking over. When I was overwhelmed by this darkness, I happened to have a call with her and I told her, "I'm not good." I couldn't stop crying. I told her the spot I was in was very, very dark and she said something that completely changed my life.

She said, "Melissa, darkness has no force of its own. It's only the absence of light," because I kept saying, "The darkness is overtaking me."

And she said, "The only thing that's happened here is you stopped shining your light. That light is yours to shine. You're choosing now not to shine it," because when I go there, I'm very tired. It's usually that life has just kept beating me up and I become extremely exhausted. The word everyone uses for depression is "exhaustion." And I just, I don't want to shine my light anymore. I just want to go to sleep and not wake up.

Then she said, "When you're ready to shine your light, all it will take is one little flame to light up that cave." When I shine my light, the darkness disappears. And when I don't shine my light, the darkness appears to take over.

I thought of it as I'm having a lull now and I'm not able to shine my light because I'm really, really tired. But if I allow myself to be in that darkness knowing that it has no force of its own, it's just my own choice to turn off my light. When I allow myself to heal and become stronger, then my light will shine again.

That was like a year ago and for the next couple days I just existed. I didn't try to do the performance. I took walks. I sort of just let myself be and something amazing happened: I started to gain my strength back and about three days later, I was back at baseline and nothing dramatic happened. I allowed it. I didn't fear it. I realized the darkness doesn't have any power—it's just my own choice to dim my light for a little while as I become stronger again. I believe if we can think about it that way, it becomes an existential choice rather than a circumstance that's just happening to us without our control.

MF: Thank you for sharing that, it is immensely helpful to talk about. I like to talk about these things because of the fact that if I can get out of the darkness, everything will function so much better. I sometimes go dark for a while and I can completely relate. It's almost like it's taken over and I know what I need to do.

MB: It's like that period of hibernation when you're just kind of going into yourself and gaining that strength back, because what you're doing is so energetically draining that if you're a feeler, you can't just do it stoically. It's going to drain your vitality and your light is going to dim and I think it's about becoming aware. Another thing I've done is I've become very aware when I feel myself going below the line.

I identify as a martyr. I serve. I have six children. I'm the person who has all of everything and I take it all on stoically because I want to be *that* person. Sadly, it's kind of one of my areas that I take pride in, but I'm older now. I'm not in my 20s anymore and I can become overwhelmed by it all really easily. Now I start to see when I'm feeling my light starting to dim and if I don't do something, it's gonna happen again. I gotta take time for myself. I'll take an extra walk today, or I'll start to take care in advance.

MF: I can either get back to above the line, or it will spin out of control. One of the words that comes up a lot of times for me is resentment, because I give to a lot of people, I have my three kids, I have my mom, my dad, my family and my resentments.

MB: Yes, well, that's a martyr. You realize a martyr sacrifices themselves to serve others and ends up bitter and resentful.

MF: Yeah and then the resentment gets out of control.

MB: That's the point where you start to become more like in Japanese culture where you are never focused on yourself. So it's ingrained in your epigenetics that you do not focus on yourself, but then you do not give yourself self-care. Me too. I come from a bunch of martyrs and it was like "Self-care is indulgent, never call attention or focus on yourself." So for me, self-care in my practice is the hardest part of it. But now I'm realizing it's the most critical thing because self-care involves boundaries, too.

And having the courage to say "I'm sorry, I can't do that. I don't have the energy." So maybe you're human, which is very hard.

MF: Self-care, absolutely. It's funny because self-care sometimes means getting a massage, but it's also things that are more subtle. My therapist now says, "Instead of labeling it—go for a run, meditate for 60 minutes or just do nothing."

MB: I wrote in a workbook on this and I've had to relabel them all so they didn't seem so indulgent. So I call those "enhancing longevity." I think about it as if I need to be a role model. I have four daughters and two sons. If I show them that life is about working yourself into the ground and not caring about yourself and prostrating yourself before others and becoming like a puddle of subservience, then that's the wrong message. I want my daughters to be strong and have boundaries and be able to say, "I deserve this." If I can't do it for myself, I do it to enhance longevity so I can be here for them. I also do it as a role model.

So sometimes when something's hard for me, I say to them, "I'm going to do this for myself. And I want you to do that, too. I want you to realize that you *do* matter, you are worth taking care of."

MF: What else do you do when you feel yourself heading down into the darkness?

MB: I'm now able to sit in it. The only way you handle it is to allow yourself to be in it and not change anything and know that it's cyclical and it's the reason we're able to do the work we do. We are able to feel it all from the lowest low to the highest high. It's about allowing yourself to breathe into it and saying, "I can be here and it's not pleasant and I don't enjoy it. In fact, I despise it, but I can be in it now. I know that it's not going to subsume me." That's what I thought was going to kill me, suffocate me. Now I realize that it's actually kind of a choice my body is making.

It's my body saying, "I'm out, sister, you're not going to keep pushing at that rate, shining your light because your light isn't eternal." Your light has limits on it. And if you want to keep shining that brightly, you're going to have to let it dim for a while, too.

I think if we become more aware, we won't go as extreme. Then we can start to dip—realize, oops, we need a little self-care, dip there, don't go way to the bottom and then move with the ebbs and flows that are a little less severe as we go.

MF: Because we want to just try to pull ourselves out. I've talked to a lot of these exited entrepreneurs, and they come to the finish line where they feel totally overwhelmed. I had one client who sold a medical company making more money than he knew what to do with. He developed this horrific skin condition that's caused by stress because he was lonely and suicidal. It seems like you considered your mental health *before* you were forced to exit. Is that true?

MB: I became a certified logotherapist, or I should say a meaning coach. My way out of my deep, dark despair was logotherapy, which is healing through meaning. There's a very prescribed path to access meaning. And one of the most critical core tenets of logotherapy is that you must believe that life has unconditional meaning in all situations and circumstances, which was the hardest thing for me to believe, because I didn't believe life had any meaning at that point.

I was a nihilist. And you know, that's when I tried to end my life, because I thought life had no meaning.

I, as a human, had no capacity to make meaning in a meaningless existence. But once I adopted logotherapy, I had to say life had unconditional meaning in all circumstances, which meant that I have my mindset, which is one of the key three cores of logotherapy—I had to develop a more optimistic mindset.

I had to stop asking "Why is this happening to me?" I had to say, "*How* is this happening *for* me in every single thing?" As opposed to saying "Figures, this would happen because life sucks and it's meaningless. You know, there is no reason for me to be here."

I had to say if life has unconditional meaning, then how am I going to find meaning in this horrible situation? I would say I started to think that way, but I truly had no idea that it would hit me as hard as it did. There was so much bitterness. There were so many things in my experience because it wasn't just selling the company and having it end. It was about being ousted from the company, of course, that I had been at for 32 years and not being able to say goodbye to any of my team. Having a guy who was running it be the devil that I wanted to kill, literally, because both Doug and I imagined ourselves beating his body to a pulp.

It was so many different things. The truth was, when I mentioned it to my wise and existential psychotherapist, she said, "But you did choose to do it, Melissa." The truth was we had made a choice to do it and we could have just as easily made a choice not to sell our company and make lots of money and buy lots of nice things earlier on.

We had chosen to do it. And one of the other things everyone else sees is that when we think about something we've left, we also only think about it in the most romantic and positive light with a revisionist history. We think about it as the days that were perfect, when everything went our way and we were in our groove and everybody was around us and we were, you know, hugging and singing kumbaya.

But the truth is, when I really thought about it, where I was after 32 years was actually not a great place. I really didn't enjoy being there anymore. We were a huge company, we had over a thousand people and we were not like an entrepreneurial company. We had to create things that the customers wanted and fire people, and people complained all the time.

The truth is, neither Doug nor I enjoyed what we were doing at all anymore. So when I looked at it realistically again and I said, "How is this happening *for* me rather than *to* me?" I said, "Oh my gosh, they freed me from a prison." And actually, if I saw this guy and had a chance to talk to him, the CEO who came in, I would probably thank him...but maybe in a sarcastic way.

But I'd say, you know, "I wanted to kill you for a good many years, but now, actually I have to thank you because you freed me from a prison and showed me that I have the capacity to do lots of other things. So thank you."

It's learning to step away from ourselves to look objectively from the outside that allows us to become more open-minded and compassionate.

MF: That perspective shift is life-changing. It's been a tough year for me caring for my mother who has Alzheimer's. The first thing I thought about was exactly what you said: "Why is this happening *to* me at this time?" But now I feel a huge shift when I change it to, "Why does this happen *for* me?" I'm so grateful I *get* to take care of my parents. My mom's 97. My dad's 89. How many of my other cousins are here without their parents? My closest cousin lost his mom and dad before 80. My other cousin lost her mom when she was 64 from breast cancer. That's why I have to remind myself that I *get* to do this. Would my cousins drop everything and probably pay a big sum of money to take their mom and dad to the doctor? Absolutely. So yes, I completely connect with that, Melissa. I can't thank you enough, this is so amazing and you are amazing.

MB: You owe it to yourself and everyone else that you know to learn how to take care of yourself, to keep shining, consistently.

I think one of the hardest things for me has been finding kindred spirits who really get this. I could never talk about this stuff with lots of people in my life because it's way too dark for them and they—even my own husband—do not respond to me with, "Same here."

But that's everything—to feel understood.

STEVE DISTANTE

Steve Distante is the chairman and founder of Vanderbilt Financial Group, the founder of ImpactU.me, a farmer, documentary filmmaker and the author of *Once Upon a Time in Entrepreneurland*.

Steve was part of my original mastermind group. I've always relied on him for advice about complicated banking matters, which is invaluable to me. He runs the Private Investor Network, an organization that does "matchmaking" for exited entrepreneurs with liquid cash looking for quality enterprises in which to invest. This matching system provides an incredible opportunity for entrepreneurs on both sides of the coin to seek true alignment.

Steve is someone who operates at an extremely high-level frequency. He has remarkable character, living his life and running his businesses with the utmost integrity. As a wealth manager, Steve recruits other high-caliber, high-character advisors to find connections that align with their values. Steve has written several books geared toward entrepreneurs. He writes in fable form, which I personally believe is the best way to speak to entrepreneurs with short attention spans and a bottom line. I love that Steve's sole purpose for writing these books is to help other entrepreneurs navigate the chaos of living within and outside of their businesses.

Steve is a documentary filmmaker, as well as an author and entrepreneur. He is the chairman and founder of Vanderbilt Financial Group focusing on sustainable wealth management. Steve is also the enthusiastic founder of ImpactU.me, a platform that educates students and professionals about Impact Investing.

STEVE DISTANTE [SD]: One of things I want to share with you on my INFJ journey is that I'm amazing at doing Clarity Blueprint sessions [a performance-based growth strategy rubric for businesses] with people where I can bring people to awareness about where they want to go and what they want to do and how to get there. It takes me about four hours of sitting with a person. I think the reason it takes four hours is because that's about how long it takes for a person to let their guard down. What I learned with my INFJ personality type is we literally can feel a person's emotion. So somebody depressed could be sitting three seats for me and I'll pick up on it and not even know it. That is both a blessing and a curse. So a lot of the ups and downs that maybe I've gone through actually weren't mine.

MARK FUJIWARA [MF]: Right. I feel that all the time, Steve. All the time. It takes one person to elevate me on the flip side, too, because I can rise with a person's energy. Somebody's coming in authentically and they've got this zest—that hooks me.

SD: And it's just like, well, I come in pretty high and I'm getting higher with that person.

MF: Yeah. I completely get it. You almost have to keep a scorecard on an hourly basis.

SD: And there's nothing wrong with you to need it. That's changed everything for me. I realized that when you sense a person's dishonesty, their jealousy, their envy, whatever it might be, everybody's transparent. When you call them out on it, they get very defensive and try to make you feel stupid. Then you realize, no, actually, I know the truth. You're just defending yourself.

MF: I get it. Exactly.

You know, Steve, I feel like you just know the senior path, the next-level way to go. You're rare because of the fact that you can follow through. To stop working altogether or stop making income altogether, it's not in my DNA and it is not in your DNA. But you're on the other side of having exited where you're just finding your *ikigai*, acknowledging there's an even higher level to this. You have the ability, combined with true *ikigai*.

SD: I have, I think, seven companies named ImpactU. It's how I define myself. I want to impact you. I want to be a gift to you. However that works. And if I can, my mission has been accomplished. And it's a huge deal because my biggest opportunities are with people who have entrepreneurial clients, but to have so many people in my life who actually are entrepreneurs —people like you—you're a whole new level.

MF: Wow. So it's a core value of yours.

SD: It's my essence. If I ever got a tattoo, that would be it: "Impact you." I've got hats. I've got shirts. I've got companies. It's just a really good reminder for me that being a gift to other people is what it's all about for me.

MF: Amazing. I work with so many exited entrepreneurs who become fish out of water when they find themselves on the other side of exiting their companies.

SD: I bet they are feeling like, "What the fuck?" Like seriously, somebody gave me the wrong rules to the game.

And so what's the new goal? When these people exit, they don't consider the fact that they have drive, that they have this risk tolerance and they need to have free will. And what's the mistake they make? Well, quite often, they decide they're going to let the evil empire PE [private equity] take over their companies, then they sign an agreement to work for that PE company, sometimes for years, and find themselves miserable as hell and leave a ton of money on the table. Does that sound familiar?

MF: Yep, exactly.

SD: It's because we're broken and we're unemployable sometimes as solo entrepreneurs. You have to ask yourself, "Do you even *like* being an entrepreneur?" This is a general question. "Do you like being an entrepreneur, or do you like having money? Or do you like votes?" Because entrepreneurship has its benefits. We're able to lead, we're able to create, we're able to do whatever we want. And I believe and have seen that a lot of entrepreneurs go into protective mode with that precious money, resource money, because now they don't have unlimited cash. But once they've exited, they now have a finite amount.

What you find is a lot of entrepreneurs who sell, get bored, get demented, from the perspective of realizing that risk is what makes them happy as people, but they're addicted to that risk so they have no outlet to turn to.

MF: The script is you sell your company. Somewhere along the line, you get the message that this is how it's supposed to be. Though that's where you are like, "Oh these are the things I'm supposed to do once I've sold." It is even more of a mental health thing when these entrepreneurs are not at all satisfied with what's being told to them. Although, it's more of what they're listening for than anything else.

SD: Yeah, I was on the phone with a billionaire recently. It was just so intense. I asked him directly: "Why is making more money so important to you?" Like, didn't you get the notification that that's not what it's all about? It's about having impact on other people, having impact on communities, individuals, being a thought leader, being able to bring people to a place they never imagined they could be. That's what life's all about. It's just so messed up because, unfortunately, we've been programmed out this way. First it's jealousy and then it's envy.

Perhaps it even devolves into schadenfreude [feeling happiness or joy watching another person fail or suffer], where they want you to basically lose it all and go to jail for it. There's great joy in that, though, thinking about someone like Martha Stewart's downfall. *Really, how does that give you joy?* In our lives, there are people who harbor resentment towards our achievements and our assets, whatever it is and I'm like, why? What's the difference? You had the same community, you had everything. It's not in your DNA. It's in *my* DNA to be driven. Because I'm an INFJ, my strengths involve being very analytical and that helps me look at the long term to put things together. Eventually, I had to find the right "who's" in my life. And that's this project, this book, this "Who Hunter" is big [referring to his book, *Pitchology: The Art & Science of Raising Capital for Entrepreneurs*].

MF: I'm very excited that you brought this up because on the private wall side, my team and I have that covered. I'm the

one that goes in and actually I'm getting to a point right now where I just said, "Hey, let's really paint the picture on the second mountain after your exit."

I don't want to work with somebody who is just like, "I want the most money and I'm on it just to make more and more and more money." That doesn't work for me. What I'm building now and one of the reasons why I went down that road is that it's very powerful to unlock your purpose. I've cracked the code on these exited entrepreneurs.

SD: Okay, how do you do that?

MF: I talk to them from an empathetic place. In our conversations, the first thing out of our mouths is that we're talking about the suicide attempts that we've made. We're talking about how scary it is to be an entrepreneur and to have mental health struggles. There's no pitch book. There's no performance reports. There's no nothing. It's just like, I know I could do a really good job for you. There's just no agenda.

SD: And it's "I know you trust me." Doesn't happen too often, but when you make those connections with people, it's really refreshing. We can call each other any time. So understanding the persona of an entrepreneur is something I do really well, being able to keep an entrepreneur's attention. The fact that you're only going to be happy when you're doing certain things and when you smile and say, "It's nice to have the money. I have the money, but I don't need to get out of my business to do it." How do you monetize throughout your career, your journey, how do you monetize? And if you had the money, would you leave your firm? Would you leave your company? Because that will probably decide whether you're really an entrepreneur or not, right? So there you go. That's the story, and I'm sticking with it. I could go on for hours. I think any exited entrepreneur could.

MF: Look, I'll be honest, I have such a big team at Baird that I don't make that much money after all the mouths are fed. First of all, you have to give 50 percent to the house. And then there are all these other people, who, by the way, make my life easier because I don't have to show up to a lot of these meetings. They have their heart in this business. But I feel like a lot of these people, they're going to add a lot of value for the client. I don't think as a financial advisor, that would be my greatest impact for someone.

SD: It's all about people being able to help other clients or entrepreneurs track what they're investing in, so they don't get taken advantage of. They are also able to be better humans to others by doing what it is that we do, which is to show people how to learn and grow using money as a tool. I feel it's very much connected to who we are as entrepreneurs and it actually helps us get that juice, that excitement in order to feel purposeful.

It's about getting honest with ourselves. The reason we do this is because we want that juice from taking a risk, and so that's why we invest and buy the businesses in the first place. The fatal error that people make is, if they're giving money to an entrepreneur, they don't create their victory conditions, and often get ghosted and they don't start with The End in mind. Then they're left with a heap of unfulfilled expectations.

MF: So, how does all this great energy and wisdom going toward entrepreneurs translate to looking after yourself? Have you found that you need to pay closer attention to your own needs as you help more and more people?

SD: I do breath work every morning and I do meditation every morning. I start my day off right. Most days I'll do a cold plunge or so, but I feel very stable and very intentional and very patient and very aligned with what I should be doing. That carries me most days.

I've had money and I've had money risk, I've had free will, and I know that I need all three of those things in my life in order to make it exciting and worth living.

But at the end of the day, I have to look after myself to be effective. We all need to be doing that for ourselves to succeed.

TODD EVENSON

Todd Evenson is the COO of Think Insurance Group, whose mission is to make healthcare affordable for every American.

Todd and I met because of a very good mutual friend of ours, Kelly Keifer. I am beyond stoked any time someone I care about, admire and respect wants me to meet someone new with those same characteristics. Kelly runs a clean energy business and because of her direct experience as an entrepreneur, she was adamant that I meet Todd. We both trust her unconditionally and I know that is how we were gifted with such a great friendship.

MARK FUJIWARA [MF]: What are your thoughts on exited entrepreneurs finding support for their unique type of situation?

Todd Evenson [TE]: I think sometimes it's hard when exited entrepreneurs get caught up in everything. We get so busy in our daily lives that we tend to drive right through what is important. I fear that we forget how connection with others is probably the best way to live our lives, at home and at work.

MF: After I first shared some of my struggles with a group of other entrepreneurs, friends of mine in the group said, "I've never seen you stronger or lighter than after those words came out."

TE: Isn't that interesting? I know exactly what you're saying in terms of having to find those dark spots in your life to reflect. I've had wild success and wild failure. I'm not convinced we know how to prepare for those extremes. Especially when you've had success all your adult life in so many ways. I think of what happens with the trap of our own making, which is the ego of the self. I'm not saying ego in terms of the negative, I'm just saying the ego of the self paints this picture of who we think we are and how we think others see us. None of it is real.

If given the space, we contemplate ourselves and our ego, then we think, *Well, what if all these people think this and what if all those people think that*? Next, we start to believe our thinking because it turns into a story we tell ourselves. Over the years, this illusion of self just keeps piling on and piling on. Ultimately, that is where I've seen a lot of my friends end up and how I knew it was true for me when I was at the height of my career. I was the least happy I had ever been and didn't even realize it. Wow! So I got out. I left that persona behind. I'm not saying it's easier on this side of things. But I don't just want to be happy. I'm not saying that. I think a lot of people have the wrong idea about the purpose of life being how happy we are. Instead, I want to be fully alive. To do that, I am clear about how: if I want to see the light, I must be willing to experience the dark.

MF: I feel you, Todd. You're so right about the ego, too, because the ego often gets in the way, blocking those conversations we need to be having.

TE: I remember how talking about mental health was considered taboo. No one wanted to say anything publicly about depression. Even when I wanted to talk about my struggles, I didn't think I could or should. But over the last couple of years, society has started to evolve. It seems like we've only evolved to the point where we are willing to say something at all. We're willing to share a little bit of the darkness we experience. And it's kind of this enlightening thing when you see people go on TV and say, "Oh, I was walking through this hard thing recently." So now it's almost fashionable to be willing to express your hardships out loud.

We as a society watch our heroes on TV and think, "Oh, the stars are letting me in to feel their pain." I'm sorry, no, Taylor Swift is not "letting you in" when she shares her story. Only those who you're close to can know the real you. I think it's that depth that is so rare to find, especially in the moments when we're feeling pain or in a particularly acute moment of need. The ability to deeply connect and communicate with the ones we trust so we are not out there alone in the abyss is what's important.

MF: As much as we might want to, we can't just watch someone randomly far out there to feel that connection for ourselves, through osmosis or something.

TE: There are lots of better things to get into, like watching birds outside instead of staring at the TV. At my mountain property, that's actually what I enjoy doing the most. The best show to watch is the light show of stars at night!

MF: When we are in a negative state, there are also these little, insidious things that happen with being around the wrong people who we are not aligned with. I feel like you have that awareness, as well.

TE: My autistic son is my best teacher. You'll hear me say that all the time. It has a lot to do with the type of communication he teaches me. Some of the things he didn't learn until much later because we didn't have the language to understand—like recognizing when he was uncomfortable or how we learned to watch his face for little micro-movements—all these sorts of things we had to figure out along the way. I had to try hard to tune into him differently to communicate better. And by the grace of God, I think that intention translates into the rest of my life.

If you're watching and paying attention, then you can have this richness of communication and sometimes not have to say anything to your colleagues or family while being able to be perfectly understood. We're able to go into these crazy spots that no one else ever talks about. Or at least feeling safe enough to explore them. We should not always have the answer, though. We should have more *questions* than answers. This posture of having the best questions versus the right answers enlightened me about the 'how' aspect of things. I had to make those changes as a person in order to communicate better.

There is no formula to figuring out better communication or deep connection, in my opinion; there is no series of checkboxes to go through. But if I show up authentically—without pretense or expectation—it allows me to find real relationships like ours. Within a minute of meeting, we understood that there was a depth of connection there between us. We knew right away! We didn't need to go further by building out trust over the years. No, I already trusted and knew the real you, Mark. Finding connections can happen that quickly. It requires that both parties show up authentically for it to happen. That's the trick. Inherently, when you've done the work to learn who you are, it makes it easy to create deep connections with others who also know themselves. It makes life a lot more blissful because you begin to seek others who are on the path of "knowing thyself" right along with you. You see they are on that journey, too. That kind of trust is deep and instantaneous. That's when you realize you are no longer alone.

MF: I look back at the people I've shared with and I see that you have that intuition going in. You're creating a certain type of environment, in terms of how to have the most authentic relationships.

TE: It's amazing how quickly those relationships form, solidify and find permanence. I hardly talk to a lot of people I'm closest to. But they also know I'm right there if they need me. When I reach out, it's never awkward, like, "Hey, how have you been?" They know I don't do small talk. I prefer to talk about substantial things. So we dig in right away. We can talk about these crazy things in business or in life, because all of that comes from the same source.

MF: I don't believe in the binary of having a work-life balance, for that matter, because there's no such thing. You're just alive.

TE: If you're in an environment that makes you feel alive, you're in a flow that connects you to the universe. Consequently, your mental health will be sound and hearty enough to be in and accept the present. As a function of this concept, I don't find suicidal ideation by business professionals all that surprising. The separation of our work and life leads to an identity crisis. Who am I? Why am I here? What is my purpose? Sadly, the loving feelings we've developed by accepting our ego selves has led to despair and disillusionment.

My truth is that business and life are inseparable. I used to do things like fly across the country for a 15-minute meeting and fly back. Because I thought my purpose was to provide for my team and my family. I was stupid. The voice in my head had this relentless, repetitive narrative: *I go to work, then after that, I get to see my son. But I should stay later at the office. I'm gonna work until midnight. Ah shit, I am a terrible father because I didn't get to see my son.* The mental and physical process repeated itself over and over again until I learned that I had to stop wishing for a future and regretting my past. I needed to be present at this exact moment. I found peace mentally and physically, which helped me find my purpose. I needed to be present in every moment. That year, I didn't miss a single one of my son's basketball games. I didn't miss a single play he acted in. I found the grace to forgive myself. I let go.

The idea of presence and grace was an entirely new approach for me. The concept of having my work life and daily life evolved into one *life*. Once entrepreneurs figure this out, that it is all just the same thing, life moves from separation and isolation to profound connection. So much of who we are as business owners is about the excitement of the risks we take. There's excitement pretty much by the second. We are constantly dealing with putting out the usual fires: "I have money, I don't have money. I should hire staff, I should fire staff." This requires high intensity and energy. The risk is to burn out—unless you are connected to something greater than yourself.

MF: There's so much good stuff there. I feel like when I'm present, I am able to have this calmness of mind. When I look back in time and I say, "Oh, wow. This happened and that happened." Then I start to re-feel things. That means I'm reliving that trauma, rather than experiencing how things are in this moment.

TE: In my mind, it's always a worst-case scenario, right? It's a wild trap. We relive the bad stuff first. We are just wired that way. Many great philosophers have explored the concept of being "in the now" or the present. I was terrible at this. I'd lay in bed every night, replaying the past day and planning for things that I thought were going to happen tomorrow. As you would expect, I hardly slept—I'm certain you and these other entrepreneurs can relate. It took a long time to mute the chatter in my mind. It took practice. Finding my peace started with my physical health. I had to burn some of the built-up tension with physical activity. Next, I started to work on my mental state. Meditation and finding quiet helped. Finally, I had to consider my energetic self. This was a completely new thing for me to contemplate. Eventually, I started to gain the capacity to change my awareness from my busy, relentless brain to find my connection to infinite and quiet. I still practice that a lot, by the way.

MF: That kind of presence helps communication in general. It teaches people how to show up as the most authentic version of themselves. When you show up in that way, where everything is intentionally geared toward growth, it almost allows you to *scale* authenticity. It's how you're able to accomplish huge shifts collectively.

TE: Yeah, I mean, there's so much richness in what you're saying and I think reflecting on the business colleagues I have, part of that authenticity is risky in and of itself. A lot of times, rightly or wrongly, it depends on the company culture, the organization and a lot of things. I've known scared CEOs who weren't willing to admit it because they were afraid to be authentic. They had worn that armor for so long. You have politics where people are constantly trying to tear you down the moment you leave the room. You're constantly in a position where somebody else is vying for your job. There's somebody else who doesn't like your opinion, and so it's that much more important to be authentic with somebody like yourself or to these exited entrepreneurs.

It's why you have 16 people on your short list of speed-dial contacts and not 1600, right? These folks have welcomed you in a way and you've welcomed them to where they can admit those things and experience the Maslow [Hierarchy of Needs]. It's safety first and to have those safe relationships, I've always said you only get a handful of relationships like that. It's hard in business because that's the opposite of what we are used to and what we are taught.

I think often about performance-based cultures. The Wall Street way, ABC players, all climbing over one another to happily help you fail and watch themselves win. When I travel to certain cities, I recognize that I'm not in Kansas anymore; I'm in the lion's den. I'm not saying that to make a value judgment. Often direct confrontation is easier because you at least get authentic reactions. But, do you feel safe? You have to be authentic to attract real authenticity. And if you haven't been willing to go there, you will automatically not be authentic to the people you are surrounded by.

I think a lot of people get trapped into thinking you have to go up this hierarchy of climbing to be successful. "I was the VP over there, so now I need to be the VP at the next job." It's all a bunch of crap, but we're caught again and again like that in our ego. Inevitably, we think our positioning is a viable measure of success. There's a different type of success out there for us if we are willing to be open to it.

As a society, I think we are becoming more enlightened about what success can look like. I give credit to the younger generations because older people learned to beat themselves up pretty badly about who they are. I know younger people have watched us as Boomers or Gen X'ers and there's something—I don't want to call it a balance—I think that's the wrong thing; there's just something more than, "Okay, I sold my business for $100 million so I'm done now." They see that there is more to the equation.

Or, "Well, I can buy whatever I want. So I'll go and buy *everything* I want." That might keep someone's attention for about six months.

Then, there's the thinking, *Now I hate myself because I'm alone.* I think about folks who have been entrepreneurs who have had a big exit. I think there's some variation here, ranging from an exit of a million, millions, or hundreds of millions. They had a network of people who they engaged with every day. The reason they were successful is because they went to the luncheons, they went to the happy hours, they went to the business meetings and boardrooms, and they had a connection with an extensive network of people, even though it was mostly business-oriented.

They got accustomed to being in the spot where there was some fulfillment in all of that. Then what happened was that they said, "Okay, well, I'm going to go from an extremely high-intensity environment to say, 'Oh, I just sold.'" I think you use the example of your buddy who wanted to try to play the senior PGA tour. How miserable! No, that's not the same energy. Like, don't get me wrong. It's pressure, but it's not the same energetic thing that you did in business that made you successful. Unless you have an unwinding pathway that you've already almost predefined, things are not going to align so easily for you.

We do this in business all the time. We say, "Well, here's my three-year strategic plan," for the entrepreneurs. I know you should plan on five years, but you need to be planning the two years before you get out first. Then three years later, you might have a chance. The timeline there takes on a life of its own.

MF: It's almost like the route you went with was against the norm. The progression was: you sell a business or you exit a business or you move on from the business, then you go to another one, then you buy another one or you find another one and you just keep repeating that process. Why? Because you saw some other guys do it. The interesting thing is that you're out of one of two things. One is that "Well, I've achieved this and I want to achieve this other goal in business." It's applying the same idea that "I had a software company, so I'm going to buy another one." Or it's the mentality that, "Oh my gosh, I'm just going to go off and do

whatever," and not think it through. But you were intentional, which is very rare.

TE: Not quite. I found the gift of being unhappy. I did my best throughout my career. I achieved the highest levels in my industry. I should have been happy. Right? Wrong. I lost my true self along the way. I just wasn't afraid to say it anymore. My progression of success had to move from some sort of business title to focus on the human I needed to become. I lost pretty much everyone close to me in the business world throughout that journey. But I learned that was just a season in my life, just like having success was. I'm grateful for what I learned.

MF: And, "Well, this was fun," but then a few things come with that kind of resignation. One is the question "Who are you doing all of this with?"

TE: You've got to ask yourself always, "Who are you doing it with?" Your friends? Your family? Your colleagues?"

MF: They're probably all still working. The other thing is, now you have to get back down to reality. So I want to applaud you because you considered all of this in your intentional exit, which was a big part of figuring out your plan ahead of time.

TE: I think the easiest way through an exit is to set the expectations of yourself ahead of time. There is a reality about how you see yourself. Part of that self is somebody who has authority, somebody who can articulate things, share visions and discuss really heady topics, with the expectation of attainment and meaning.

I had to be ready to say, "Wait a minute, even if I go into board meetings, I'm just gonna be me," and it is somewhat disconcerting to the people who are in the room sometimes. They aren't ready for what I have to say. I mean, I'll lean straight in. I'll talk about religion, I'll talk about gender, I'll talk about race, I'll talk about all these things that might make them uncomfortable. I do not have the same filter I once did.

I've been lucky. While exiting my "old self" and "old life" I was serving as a Board Chair for a Community Mental Health center. It provided me with several authentic relationships with professionals I could lean on for help. I finally got to find myself by being real with them. These are the relationships that I maintain today because I've finally found my peace.

MF: I consider how we serve others to be the most effective tool to help with mental health issues. In certain situations, you need medication depending on the condition(s) you're dealing with. But for me at least, I got a lot of hope once I began to meet people who I could share my experience with safely. Being of service to others has a hugely positive impact on mental health.

TE: Yeah, we live in a hard world. I mean, there's so much judgment. I think this was maybe another thing I had to figure out on those long bike rides by myself after I exited. It was the fact that I'm not the judge. In our roles, we have to make decisions as CEOs. We have to shoot from the hip and we have to put the game face on that we have the answer. And the truth is, we're mostly full of it and we're just doing our best. We're scared as hell. That's the truth. We're scared as hell. The grace we had in our careers is that we had good timing. We caught a lucky break. We got to know the right person who opened doors for us. But in general, hardly anybody in the world has ever been the CEO of Facebook, so how do you train to be that? You don't. You don't, so you have to figure it out on the job.

MF: My ideal outcome for this book is to help exited entrepreneurs see that and to dramatically help their mental health in every possible way.

TE: Yes. That's why conversations like these are so meaningful. The world will take all of this in and give you lots of love back. Connections like ours pay dividends.

SHAWN JOHANSON

Shawn Johanson is the founder and CEO of Sona Investments, Inc., a multi-million dollar real estate investment firm.

I feel incredibly blessed that our friend Randy introduced us. I still remember our very first call—I was in an Airbnb with my family in Wisconsin for the weekend, parked right in the middle of the living room. From the moment we started talking, I felt an instant connection. Instead of diving into what we do for work, we skipped all that and went straight into real, vulnerable conversation. That's rare. And I knew right then that we were going to be lifelong friends.

Shawn's business, Sona Investments, creates wealth while improving industrial properties, office buildings and retail centers throughout the United States. Shawn and his partners identify commercial properties in need of revitalization, and then begin to implement strategies that lead to the acquisition of equity, rapid growth and solid investment returns.

When we first spoke, Shawn shared something he hadn't shared with many people. He assumed that once he hit his financial goals—milestones that are supposed to bring freedom and joy—he was overcome with anxiety. It built up to the point that he passed out on a plane. He was miserable and didn't understand why. He had the belief that once money came easily, happiness would soon follow. Once it became clear that wasn't the case, it was terrifying.

I told Shawn about other business owners who had a similar experience, people who had "made it." They ended up lost, and depressed, some even teetering on the edge of taking their own lives because the emptiness after the exit was just that overwhelming. It was one of those moments where you realize: we're not alone. There's this unspoken crisis happening behind the polished success stories, and we need to talk about it.

MARK FUJIWARA [MF]: I know you're in the process of creating and moving through your bucket list. Can you tell me more about it?

Shawn Johanson [SJ]: Yeah, my wife and I are using an EOS —Entrepreneurial Operating System—not just in business, but in our personal lives, too. We've been having intentional conversations about everything we want to experience and create. Right after she exited her business, Janet committed to saying "no" to everything for the first year just to give herself space.

We've thrown around the idea of buying businesses and installing teams to run them—kind of a private equity-style model but with a twist. We want to lead with values and protect culture, which we believe is the core of a successful business. Traditional private equity often overlooks that, and it's something we don't want to compromise.

But honestly, nothing's set in stone yet. We're just exploring.

When I was at Business Mastery with Tony Robbins, I found myself thinking way more about dyslexia than about business. That was a big sign. Both my daughter and I have dyslexia, and that calling just keeps getting louder. It feels like this is the work I'm meant to do right now.

All of my Tony Robbins experiences have been powerful. They've helped me reconnect deeply—with my daughters, with Janet and with myself. It's brought so much clarity and happiness into our lives. Janet and I have grown closer through this journey. We are having more intentional conversations, dreaming bigger and supporting each other in ways we hadn't before. I'm finally moving toward things that used to feel out of reach because of old self-limiting beliefs. I'm just really grateful for the progress, for the connection and for where life is leading us.

MF: What is it about dyslexia that drives you to take action?

SJ: I want to connect the people doing amazing work in the dyslexia space and share a bigger vision. But first, I need to immerse myself in the dyslexic community—to see what's already out there and what's missing.

From what I've seen so far, there are three major problems. First is awareness and education. It took two years to figure out what was going on with my daughter, London. Timing and resources were everything. Now imagine kids in low-income families, where parents or caregivers are working two or three jobs who don't have time or access to those same resources.

Here's the idea: let's create targeted ads for Pre-K and kindergarten parents—and teachers—showing them what dyslexia looks like. Not just the stereotypes, but the subtle signs, too. Something like: *"Here's what you thought dyslexia looked like...but it can also look like this."* Then a call to action: *"Think your child might be showing signs? Click here for more info."* That leads to a site with helpful tools—maybe even a quick screener. It's not a diagnosis, but it gets parents closer to clarity.

Step two is getting a proper diagnosis. That's our second big problem. Ours cost $2400. That's out of reach for so many families. My mom never could've afforded that. She would've tried, but it just wouldn't have been possible. So where are the grants? Where are the affordable school-based options? Schools need to be part of the solution. Teachers are the first line of defense— they're with the kids all day. They need to be trained to spot the signs early.

And then step three: getting support once the child is diagnosed. Most public school IEPs [Individualized Education Programs] just aren't built to teach dyslexic kids the way they need to be taught. Education shouldn't be one-size-fits-all. Sure, everyone needs to learn how to read, write and do basic math. But after that, let's lean into what kids are naturally great at. That's how you keep them engaged. That's how you help them thrive.

Also, many kids with dyslexia—like 20 to 30 percent—have ADHD or other co-occurring diagnoses. But most schools only treat those surface-level issues. We need to find schools that are doing this right, even if it's just a few campuses, and help them scale.

When I was at Business Mastery, our team built a business concept around dyslexia. Then we expanded it to all so-called "learning disabilities." But I said, "It's not a disability. It's a learning advantage." Most dyslexic kids have high IQs, but because they can't read well, they start to believe they're stupid. That's heartbreaking.

So to me, this is about changing the language. It's not, "I'm sorry this happened to you," but more like, "This is awesome. This is your superpower. Let's figure out how to unlock it. We'll help you with the reading, but maybe that challenge is what reveals your brilliance in math or creativity or innovation."

That's why I want to build a website that gives parents and teachers everything they need, starting with identifying the signs of dyslexia, then offering a list of grants or lower-income options for diagnoses and finally providing a directory of schools that teach dyslexic kids the way they learn best, or solid resources for homeschooling. I want to simplify the entire process—from confusion to clarity, all in one place.

MF: I understand what you mean about wanting to take action, not treating such an important issue like it's a charity. I also really resonate with something like dyslexia being considered a superpower. I think you're finding that elusive sweet spot in the entrepreneurial world. I would say you're doing exactly the right thing, which is to go where your heart is leading you. Then the people that you'll help will be part of that continued manifestation.

Once you operate through your higher purpose, people you need to know are going to come into your world.

SJ: Yeah, that speaks to me. I think back to when I started flipping houses. I'm a terrible handyman—I hate that stuff. I don't want to be on my knees doing tile or crawling under a sink. That's just not me. But that didn't mean I couldn't be in the business. I just hired people who are great at it. One of my close friends is an incredible carpenter—25 years in the trade—but he's afraid to go out on his own. I keep telling him my story: "You're thinking too small. You don't have to do everything yourself. Just build the team, plan for that in your budget, and go."

It's the same with my reading. I don't read like most people do, and that used to hold me back. But now, I use tools—Grammarly for emails and ChatGPT when I need to polish something. It's like when email first came out no one said, "Nah, I'll just walk a handwritten letter to your house instead." You use the tools around you. That's what they're there for. You're not supposed to be good at everything—and that's okay.

My mission now is to reach kids *before* they start believing they're stupid. That's where I want to focus first. And at the same time, I want to support the older kids—like my daughter—who are already struggling with self-esteem. But I feel like if I can stop the bleeding early, we can go back and heal the damage too. That's where I feel I can make the biggest difference right now.

And honestly, this passion has only grown as I've done the inner work. Not just around dyslexia, but also around helping others see the bigger picture. At my recent real estate conference in Cleveland, I shared your story at least three or four times—the part about feeling suicidal after exiting your business. That hit people hard. It shows what happens when someone isn't mentally and emotionally prepared for what comes after "success."

I've been there, too. I got to a point where I had money and the business, but I felt miserable. And I want to help younger entrepreneurs avoid that same trap. I tell them: "Build your business, sure, but also build your emotional wealth. Understand early that money isn't going to make you happy. What it can give you is time—the time to do what matters to you."

If I can help someone in their 20s or 30s realize that now—

while they're growing their capital stacks and chasing the dream
—then maybe, just maybe, they won't have to hit rock bottom at
47 like I did. That's what drives me right now.

**MF: That almost brings me to tears because it's so real, man.
I'm starting to talk more to these people where there's this
specific commonality. So many exited entrepreneurs had the
preconceived notion that when they hit a specific valuation, or
whatever valuation exit net worth, it would be all bundled
into one.**

**They'd say, "Well, everybody says, 'When you get to this
point, you can do whatever you want and you're going to be so
happy and calm and free.'"**

**Then part of the inevitable depression and anxiety that
occurs is from the fact that you're like, "Wait, is this it? I've
reached the pinnacle and it's kind of dragging me down."**

**It's like, "I should be up here. But I'm right here down
below."**

SJ: Exactly. You hit a growth ceiling. The whole journey,
you've been driven by growth—setting goals, chasing them,
pushing forward. Then suddenly, you exit...and you're like,
"Now what?"

Sure, you can buy another business, jump back in and keep
trying to scratch that itch—seeking significance, seeking
certainty. But it doesn't land the same. I use the analogy of the
astronauts who walked on the moon. They trained their entire
lives for that one goal. And when they got there...they came back
and spiraled. Because how do you top walking on the moon?
That was their ultimate peak—and after that, they had no new
purpose. A lot of them turned to drugs or alcohol to fill
that void.

That's what happens when all your meaning is tied to achieving. If you keep raising the bar, and you keep hitting those bars,
eventually there will be no more bars. And that's when you have
to confront what *truly* matters.

At that point, you've got a few paths. One, you can start something new and try to keep chasing goal after goal. But that won't bring real happiness, because you're still in that loop. And for some, that leads to dark thoughts, even suicide.

Or, you choose to change. You redefine what happiness means. And for me, that starts with love and connection—the real kind—conversations like this, being present with your family, deepening relationships. And the second piece is contribution. Asking: "How can I give back? How can I help others avoid this same pain? What can I create that makes a difference in the thing I care most about?"

That's where the real fulfillment begins.

MF: The core of our conversation is that whatever our hearts are going towards—and you sparked something when you started talking about this—you start to recognize the fire in our own eyes and the impact of heart and soul going into something. I want to elevate that for others. I want to elevate them as much as possible.

What are the steps that you're taking to claim this big higher purpose?

SJ: When I was at Business Mastery, a few things clicked for me. Maybe it was timing, maybe I was just finally ready to hear it—but the way they broke things down into bite-sized chunks helped me metabolize it in a whole new way. That was the shift.

Once I got clear on the three main pillars of what I wanted to do, it felt like I finally had a runway. Before that, I was just stuck at the gate—waiting, organizing, trying to get everyone on board. But now, I'm cleared for takeoff. I've got vision, clarity and the focus to be intentional about how I move forward.

One commitment I've made is to fully embrace RPM—not Revenue Per Mille, but Tony Robbins' Rapid Planning Method—so I can keep growing with purpose. I've been working on setting up my categories, creating my outcomes and getting the system dialed in. That's been my top priority.

The second step is leaning into video. You and I already do that—those short video messages we send back and forth are powerful. And I've started doing that with others too, just checking in, sending a message and getting responses like, "Man, I really needed that today." It's been a simple but powerful way to connect.

And the third step is launching my *YouTube* channel. Someone at Business Mastery challenged me to start documenting this journey—not to make it about business or everything else I'm doing, but to focus it squarely on this mission: making a real difference in the world of dyslexia. Sharing the steps, the breakthroughs, the tools…and the heart behind it all.

That's where I'm headed, clear, focused and all in.

MF: That's where I am, too. And that's a great strategy.

SJ: Yeah, those are the two main things I'm focusing on right now. I've also added this mission to our EOS framework, so it's not just a passion—it's a priority. I'm on the lookout for a great podcast on dyslexia, and I've started building a reading list. I want to listen, learn and really sharpen my understanding.

I know what dyslexia looks like for me. I know what it looks like for my daughter. But I also know there's so much more to it. I want to be able to speak intelligently and confidently—not just from experience, but backed by knowledge and facts that stick with me.

Facts like this: 46 percent of inmates have dyslexia. One in five kids has it, but only 20 percent ever get diagnosed. And more than half of the people working at NASA are dyslexic. Those kinds of facts light me up because they reframe the narrative. They show that dyslexia isn't a limitation—it's a different way of thinking that, in the right environment, can become a massive strength.

What I see is this fork in the road that most dyslexic kids eventually face. One path says, "You're not good enough, you'll never amount to anything."

The other says, "Watch me—I'm going to prove you wrong."

I took that second path, and now I want to help as many kids as I can do the same.

I want to provide these kids with all the help they need to show them that they are not broken—they are brilliant, and they are worth fighting for.

ISABELLE TIERNEY

Isabelle Tierney is the founder and CEO of Choice Point and the founder of The Stress Reset. She is a Licensed Marriage and Family Therapist with nearly 30 years of experience in her practice.

Isabelle is a member of my former mastermind group, Epic Fit. The moment I heard her share with the group, it immediately hit home that she had the expertise and ability to speak eloquently about the specific issues exited entrepreneurs face.

Every time I have the opportunity to speak with Isabelle, I am blown away by her awareness and ability to pinpoint behaviors that lead to adverse mental health issues. Isabelle provides stress management tools and solutions for individuals and companies alike.

MARK FUJIWARA [MF]: A common theme I'm noticing is that exited entrepreneurs often feel misunderstood. Many struggle with a sense of unhappiness, believing that without their business, they no longer have a purpose. What common characteristics do you see in exited entrepreneurs or entrepreneurs in general? Is there a specific personality type? Are they naturally more prone to taking risks? What have you observed?

ISABELLE TIERNEY [IT]: There are some common traits. But beyond personality, there are also deep-rooted influences from childhood that shape an entrepreneur's drive. This is the classic nature-versus-nurture conversation.

On the nature side, many entrepreneurs are naturally driven, willing to take risks and drawn to innovation. Unlike someone who prefers a stable paycheck, they are often more comfortable with uncertainty and change. Many entrepreneurs are highly creative and have a strong vision, one that they feel compelled to bring to life.

But then, there's the nurture side—how childhood experiences shape their entrepreneurial spirit. Many grew up in environments where perfectionism was expected or where they had little control over their circumstances. For some, starting a business became a way to regain that control—especially over their income and their future.

Many entrepreneurs also have a deep desire to serve, to make a difference in the world. Often, this stems from childhood wounds—experiences of emotional, physical or even sexual abuse. It's almost as if they are trying to rewrite their own story: "I don't want others to go through what I went through, so I will build something that helps people."

For many, entrepreneurship is not just about success—it's about healing. Their past experiences fuel their drive to create something meaningful.

Another key trait I see in entrepreneurship is *impulsivity*. Entrepreneurs make decisions quickly, often taking risks others wouldn't. Over time, experience teaches them when to be cautious, but in the beginning, impulsivity is a huge part of the journey. It's one of those traits that is both a *gift and a curse*—it's what makes entrepreneurship possible, but it can also lead to burnout or reckless decision-making.

And that's really the key takeaway: the very traits that make someone a successful entrepreneur can also become their greatest obstacles. The ability to push through challenges, take risks and stay driven is what fuels success, but if left unchecked, these same qualities can lead to exhaustion, stress and unsustainable choices.

MF: That makes sense, especially in the context of preparing to sell the business or preparing to relinquish control in some way. I think it would be really difficult for somebody to do that.

IT: Let's talk about the gift and the curse aspect of it. For many of us, our business is not just something we built—it's something we've dedicated a lifetime to. It represents our purpose, our vision and for some, even the reason we believe we are here on this earth.

Over time, this mission becomes more than just meaningful work—it becomes our identity. And often, everything else in life takes a backseat to it. The challenge is that while this deep sense of purpose is a gift, it can also become a trap. Our identity shifts from *I have created* something successful to *I am* the success. Instead of seeing wealth, impact or recognition as something we experience, we start equating it with who we are.

This is where the gift and curse come into play. If your business was built from a deep sense of soul-driven purpose, then selling it or stepping away can feel liberating. You may think, *My mission will continue, even if I'm not the one leading it.* That's an exciting, fulfilling transition.

But if ego is wrapped up in it—if your identity is entirely tied to your role—then the separation becomes painful. You don't just lose a business; you lose your sense of self. And when that happens, what you're left with is an identity crisis because for years, everything about who you were was built around this one role.

MF: I want to go back to something you mentioned earlier. If an exited entrepreneur isn't applying that perfectionism to work anymore, where does that energy go? Where *should* it go?

IT: I'm actually going to answer with my own experience. I'm a perfectionist and there are not many places in which I am not trying to be perfect. So for me, it was business and then it was my body, right? I struggled with an eating disorder for a long time. That's the way I processed my childhood wound. And so I was always trying to have the perfect body for some people. This used to be so much more of a thing for women specifically, but now men experience it, too, with lifting weights and working out excessively.

The truth is, perfectionism doesn't disappear—it just shifts to another area of life. Entrepreneurs are wired to push, to optimize, to refine. Once the business is gone, that energy still needs somewhere to go.

I see this play out in different ways. Some people channel

their perfectionism into their physical health—becoming obsessive about diet, exercise or appearance. Others direct it toward hobbies—like wine collecting, golf or competitive pursuits. Some shift it into relationships, trying to manage or control their family and personal life with the same intensity as they once ran their business.

But here's the deeper question: "Is my perfectionism serving me or is it hurting me?" Selling a business is a rare opportunity to pause and reassess patterns that have shaped your life. It's a moment to ask, "Which values helped me succeed? Which values no longer serve me? What did I sacrifice along the way?"

Many entrepreneurs realize they gave up far more than they intended—time with family, deep friendships and even their health. And now, for the first time in years, they have a chance to course-correct.

That's why I see this phase as one of the most exciting moments in a person's life. If an exited entrepreneur approaches it consciously rather than blindly repeating old patterns, it can be transformational.

Instead of asking, "What do I do now?" The more powerful question is "How do I want to deliberately create this next chapter of my life, instead of reacting out of habit?"

MF: The reactivity part is interesting. It goes along in my mind with impulsivity being one of those gifts and curses. I am curious if you've come across anyone who, assuming they've sacrificed some of those things, or even just one of the things, in their pursuit to get to the top. What role does money play in that? Do you find that people are daunted by having all that money or does it give them freedom? Or does it cause bigger problems?

IT: So you're asking what happens when someone suddenly finds themselves with a huge pile of money in front of them? It's fascinating because right now, I'm deeply exploring the consciousness of money—what it really means, how we relate to it and how we choose to use it. Money isn't just currency; it's a reflection of our values and beliefs.

When someone exits their business and suddenly has millions at their disposal, they're faced with the huge question of, "Do I want to become a consumer? Do I start spending, buying and accumulating because I finally can? Do I want to contribute? Do I use this wealth in a way that's aligned with my deeper purpose?"

Having a lot of money requires a lot of responsibility and if someone isn't prepared for that, it can unravel them. We see this all the time with lottery winners—they come into a windfall, but because they've never examined their beliefs about money, they lose it all within a few years.

Entrepreneurs are no different. If they haven't taken the time to ask themselves, "What does money mean to me? How do I want to use it?" Then they can quickly fall into destructive spending patterns, or worse, feel completely lost despite having everything they thought they wanted.

MF: I noticed you used the word "value." I had a conversation recently with an exited entrepreneur about how he valued his time. He put a value, a monetary value, on his time. He went on to explain that he is not going to spend that kind of money or time if he doesn't feel fulfilled. But if a person sees their value as being a business owner and then that identity is gone, is it possible for them to find value in another way?

IT: There are moments in life when we are given an extraordinary opportunity and sometimes, that opportunity feels more like a crisis than a gift. Selling a business is one of those inflection points. It forces entrepreneurs to face themselves and ask, "Who am I now? How do I want to live?"

Most entrepreneurs have been like a high-speed train, moving relentlessly forward for years, often sacrificing so much along the way. When they suddenly stop, the stillness is jarring. And if they haven't taken the time to clarify their values beforehand, it can be deeply unsettling.

That's why support is critical during this phase. Without it, people can either fall into meaningless distractions—spending, consuming, jumping into another business—or they can spiral into a sense of purposelessness.

Here's the thing: *You don't have to become a saint after selling your company.* You don't have to suddenly dedicate your life to philanthropy or start a foundation. You just have to make conscious choices.

Some people choose to master a hobby—maybe they want to be the best golfer in their community. Others want to reconnect with family or travel the world. The specific choice doesn't matter as much as how they make it.

I always encourage my clients to step back and ask themselves, "What truly brings me peace, joy and fulfillment? What feels like an obligation versus a real desire? How can I live deliberately, rather than by default?" The answers are different for everyone but the key is making these choices consciously rather than just filling the void with whatever is easiest.

MF: This sounds a lot like recovery. And it seems like this type of entrepreneurial mind would be someone who can stick to a plan, or at the very least, a deadline.

IT: Absolutely. But the real question is, "Is the cost high enough?"

We all know this—whether we're talking about addiction recovery, professional burnout or major life transitions. Even for people like me, who aren't in a 12-step program, it often takes a crisis before we finally do the deep inner work. And that's true even if we have a growth mindset.

So how do we reach entrepreneurs before they hit that crisis point? How do we communicate to them, *Hey, don't waste the next one or two years spinning in uncertainty. The best thing you can do right now is start the repair process—so you don't have to suffer through the fallout later.*

This could be a preventative approach, helping entrepreneurs avoid some of the emotional and behavioral consequences that often emerge after selling their business. Because this transition is a highly vulnerable time, and when people suddenly have a space where their work used to be, that's when unhealthy coping mechanisms tend to emerge. Nature abhors a vacuum [or *horror vacui* in Latin, a concept most frequently attributed to Aristotle].

The void left behind isn't just symbolic, it's real and powerful. In that space, many entrepreneurs start grasping for something to fill it—whether that's excessive spending, compulsive new ventures, addiction or unhealthy distractions.

MF: It seems like you're describing a misalignment in a way. It's not like these exited entrepreneurs are doing bad things, but the misalignment becomes so significant for them that they start to feel like they have to perform simply for the right to exist.

IT: Exactly. I think that's part of what you're doing with these entrepreneurs, to show people a map before they even get to the point where they realize they *need* a map. "Here, this is how other people have traveled. These are the pitfalls that other people have encountered. Here are some stories both from people who've gone through it and from people who help them get through it."

Because without a roadmap, they'll struggle to find direction. But if we can say to them, "Here's how others have navigated this transition. Here are the challenges they faced. Here's what worked—and what didn't," then they won't feel as lost and alone in the process.

That's the value of hearing stories from both perspectives. Those who have gone through it and those who have helped others successfully transition.

MF: That's so relatable. Seeing that these other high-functioning people are faltering or being really open with their struggles and their mistakes, shows there is freedom in being honest. They had to turn that part of themselves off for the business for so long. I could see that causing a "come down" in a way, just like people experience getting off of drugs. It could stem from the adrenaline peaks and valleys.

IT: Absolutely. And this is why vulnerability, transparency and openness are so valuable—and why I do the work that I do.

I work best with people who are willing to be open or at least willing to learn how to be. Because let's be honest, if you're a highly successful entrepreneur, it's easy to ignore your emotional world in favor of driving your business forward.

But here's the problem: all of that accumulates. For years, entrepreneurs have pushed aside their emotions, sacrificed their well-being and neglected certain parts of their lives, all in the name of success. But when they step away from their business, all of that bottled-up energy suddenly bubbles to the surface. And that's when they start grappling with everything they didn't address before.

And as you said, when people don't have a sense of purpose, they often don't know what to do with themselves. Which leads me to my question for you: How often are you seeing addiction as a post-exit challenge for these entrepreneurs? From what I've observed, when people don't know how to fill the void, they start searching for anything to numb it.

MF: I'd say of those I've interviewed, maybe in about 50 percent of people.

IT: That's incredible.

MF: And honestly, it's probably even higher if we account for the people who haven't hit rock bottom yet—or who don't even realize they're in an unhealthy cycle.

IT: That makes complete sense.

If we go deeper into this, using spiritual language, what's

really happening is that their business has been feeding the ego. For years, they've relied on external status, success and validation to feel fulfilled. And in doing so, they've cultivated what I call "false good habits," patterns that feel rewarding in the moment but ultimately leave them empty.

These false good habits act like false gods. Money can be one, but it's not always. Success can be another. Fame, recognition, external achievement—these are all things that seem fulfilling on the surface but don't truly nourish the soul. So when an entrepreneur loses all of that, it creates an emotional vacuum. And just like with addiction, if they don't have something real to fill that space, they'll start grasping for whatever they can find.

They keep trying to fill the hole, but nothing works—because that hole was never meant to be filled with external things in the first place. That's why, to me, this transition is an exciting time—because it's the first real opportunity for an entrepreneur to finally connect with what fulfills them.

This is where the work begins—not with filling the void with another external thing, but by filling it with something real. Some people call that God. Some call it soul work. Some just call it deep inner peace. Whatever language you use, the truth is the same:

This isn't just about exiting a business—it's about rediscovering yourself.

MF: I wish that everybody had some kind of blueprint or plan or therapeutic modality to use in their lives. I wish that was available to everybody and that they *knew* it was available to them.

IT: That's exactly why I created my Stress Reset Methodology. I presented it in January [2025] at the Transformational Leadership Council, which is [*Chicken Soup for the Soul* author] Jack Canfield's group.

What makes this methodology so powerful is that it can be used on multiple levels. At the most practical, scientific level, it helps people recognize when they are in a stress response and teaches them how to assess then access their relaxation response. This alone can be life-changing in helping people navigate life's challenges. At a deeper spiritual level, it helps people recognize when they are disconnected from their soul, from God or from their deeper truth and provides a way to reconnect.

The beauty of it is that it meets people where they're at. If someone is just looking for a simple way to reduce stress, they can use it that way. But if they're searching for something deeper, it can take them to, "Oh, I've been disconnected from my soul, and that's why I feel this way."

One of my biggest goals is to make this methodology more widely available so that anyone—whether they're burnt out, overwhelmed or in transition—has access to a tool that works.

MF: One of the things that stuck with me was when you first talked to me about checking in on that scale from your methodology that goes from one (most stressed) to ten (most relaxed). I feel like every exited entrepreneur, myself included, talks a lot about mental health and the importance of preventing a downward spiral. Because once you start slipping into that spiral, it invariably leads to panic attacks, suicidal thoughts, feeling like you're not enough or feeling like you're not showing up the way you want to.

Can you talk more about how that downward spiral happens and how to stop it?

IT: Absolutely. That downward spiral you're describing is incredibly real and incredibly common, especially for exited entrepreneurs who are suddenly left without their typical structure, stimulation and sense of purpose. From a neurological standpoint, what's happening is that the brain is defaulting to a well-rehearsed stress response.

I like to use the metaphor of Olympic luging. Imagine a neural pathway—a reaction pattern, a stress loop, a way of thinking—as a luge track. Every time you engage in that loop—

pushing past your limits, obsessing over productivity or spiraling into self-criticism—you're reinforcing that track. Eventually, the moment you hit a trigger, you're flying down that icy chute before you're even aware of it.

And trying to stop that luge mid-run? Almost impossible. Your mind is racing, your heart is pounding and your behavior is on autopilot. That's what a full-blown stress spiral feels like. And to make matters worse, the brain reinforces these patterns with something called myelin sheathing. It's like putting a tunnel over that luge track—making it even more automated and harder to escape (not to mention incredibly claustrophobic).

This is what so many exited entrepreneurs experience. They've wired their systems for high-stakes, high-output performance. But once the business is gone, those same stress patterns keep firing, except now without the familiar reward or direction. That's why panic attacks, burnout or even depression can feel like they show up overnight.

So how do we stop the spiral, especially when it feels like it's happening automatically, without warning? That's exactly what The Stress Reset Methodology is designed for. It's a simple three-step process:

1. Stop
2. Slow Down and Breathe
3. Go (Choose a New Pathway)

If you realize you're heading into the stress response, whether that's anxiety, frustration or overwhelmedness, the first step is to pause. Even if you can't immediately shift to a healthier state, just stopping yourself from going further down the luge track is already a victory.

Once you stop, the next step is to breathe deeply, especially into the lower abdomen. Why? Because deep breathing signals safety to the nervous system. It's like opening the tunnel above the luge track—allowing a moment of space, a moment of possibility. And creating this space is everything. It's what allows you to make a new choice instead of going down the old, reactive pathway.

Lastly, neuroplasticity enters into the equation. Every time you choose a different reaction, a new neural pathway begins to form. At first, this is a slow process. Think of it like trying to create a new luge track: the ice is rough, the turns aren't smooth and it takes effort to steer.

Maybe you're used to reacting to stress by shutting down or lashing out. Instead, you go for a walk, text a trusted friend or put your hand on your heart and take three breaths. It might feel awkward or ineffective at first, but that one choice is the beginning of a new track.

Over time, the more you use that new pathway, the deeper and smoother it becomes until eventually, it becomes your default track. This is not an instant process. Think about braces on teeth—it takes two years to shift the position of your teeth. Why would we expect our brain—which is made of matter, just like our teeth—to change instantly? It doesn't work that way. The brain takes time to rewire, but the key is consistency.

That's why I always tell people: have grace for yourself. If you're trying to break a habit that's been reinforced for years, it's going to take time. But the good news is that every time you stop yourself from going down the old path, you're already changing the trajectory of your brain.

Sometimes, we have those breakthrough moments where we hear something or experience something that shifts things instantly. But for the most part, this is a slow, steady process and that's okay. Because every step you take toward changing your neural pathways is a step toward changing your life.

MF: There are no shortcuts, essentially. Because what you're describing seems complicated, but also very simple. When we're dealing with high-achieving people who are used to working really, really hard and throwing their weight

behind something and then being rewarded for it, how difficult is it to recalibrate their brain's reward center?

With your methodology, when you put that together, you
already had your business and clientele, right? Have you
noticed that a different type of person is now drawn to your
work?

IT: Great question. Let's start with the recalibration of the
brain's reward system because it's a real challenge and one that's
often underestimated.

High-achieving entrepreneurs are used to getting dopamine
hits from *doing*—from achieving, building and producing results.
Their entire reward system has been wired to respond to external
success: the next milestone, the next deal, the next "win." So
when that structure disappears after an exit, the brain is
suddenly starved of its usual sources of stimulation
and validation.

Recalibrating that system means learning to find reward in
entirely new ways—*not* from external achievement, but from
internal states like presence, peace, connection and well-being.
At first, that can feel unsatisfying, even disorienting. The brain is
craving the intensity and reliability of old patterns, but the new
sources of fulfillment are slower, quieter and more subtle.

This is where the methodology comes in. It doesn't ask
people to stop being who they are—it helps them *retrain* the
nervous system and the brain to respond to different cues. Over
time, the "high" doesn't have to come from a big deal closing or
a 70-hour work week. It can come from alignment, from being in
the Green Zone, from relational intimacy or from deep impact
that doesn't burn you out.

It's not an overnight process, but the good news is that the
same discipline and focus that helped them succeed in business
can be used to build a more sustainable, fulfilling life. They just
need a new playbook.

As for your next question, when I created The Stress Reset
methodology, I had already built a successful one-on-one

therapy practice. But I quickly saw that this work wasn't just for individuals. It could—and should—extend to the business world, particularly for leaders and organizations that care about their people.

So I made the intentional shift from B2C to B2B. I started working with companies, HR leaders and executives who understood that supporting the human side of business is essential, not just for well-being, but for performance. Because stress doesn't just affect individuals, it affects culture, communication and the bottom line.

Today, my work includes B2C programs for individuals who want to transform their relationship with stress; B2B partnerships with people-centric organizations who want to build resilient, high-functioning teams; transformational group programs where deep change happens in the community; a certification program that equips leaders, coaches and facilitators to bring this work into their communities.

And as I've continued on this path, I've noticed that the type of person drawn to this work has shifted. More and more, it's high-performing individuals—often exited entrepreneurs—who are ready for something deeper. They've achieved external success, but they want internal alignment. They want to lead from wholeness, not just hustle.

They're tired of pushing. They're tired of pretending everything is fine. They want tools that are practical but profound—tools that help them recalibrate not just their nervous system, but their entire way of living and leading.

What I've learned is this: these entrepreneurs are incredibly capable of doing the work. They just need a map and permission to slow down long enough to follow it. Because this isn't just about personal transformation anymore. It's about how we lead. It's about how we create. It's about how we build cultures where people thrive.

The same stress patterns I once helped individuals shift are the very same ones I now see across leadership teams and entire organizations. And that's what expanded my mission from personal mastery to leadership mastery, from internal regulation to large-scale cultural change.

At its core, it all comes down to this: when we learn to relate to stress differently, we gain access to everything that truly matters: clarity, presence, connection and impact.

I imagine that's how all of us want to live our lives.

JAY JACOBS

Jay Jacobs is the co-founder of Paperless Parts, the former CEO and founder of RAPID, a prototype manufacturer and creator of Airfield Place, a fitness, recovery, health and longevity business located in seacoast New Hampshire.

I met Jay through my former mastermind co-founder, Justin. He is an exited entrepreneur whose higher purpose is evident in everything he does. I got to know Jay better through a group call arranged by my coach, and he seemed like someone I could connect with. His intelligence and business savvy are extraordinary. And as a longevity enthusiast, he is also my favorite person to call to get good advice on cold plunges.

Jay owned a manufacturing company and after the exit saw an opportunity in something that was really fun: entering Airfield Place, the premier seacoast New Hampshire community of cutting-edge fitness, recovery, health and longevity, a 65000-square-foot state-of-the-art facility.

MARK FUJIWARA [MF]: Something I've always admired about you is your sense of clarity, especially in the business decisions you make. How do you achieve that?

JAY JACOBS [JJ]: This is my pitch for clarity in decision making: say that you need to fire a person in your company, but you procrastinate. You know it's the right thing to do, and after you do it, you're like, "Oh, why didn't I do this sooner?" What you needed to have clarity is you need to have an existing direction in life—maybe not purpose per se, but a real solid direction. That's probably what you sense in me—that clarity that shows me I'll get to where I want and need to be. Subsequent decisions tend to align with the direction I'm already going, no matter what type of decision I find myself having to make.

MF: My antennae went up last year when I started talking to exited entrepreneurs who were struggling with their mental health. I got into a kind of mini mastermind get-together, and everyone there was an exited entrepreneur except one. One

guy said, "I feel like all my friends left me. It feels like they didn't know how to act in front of me." And because he was struggling, he didn't feel comfortable going to his friends to say, "Hey, I'm depressed."

The one guy that didn't exit, I think it was like a $2 billion medical company, he said, "Yeah, I'm not exiting because I'm worried I'll end up like these other guys."

JJ: But that's like putting your head in the sand and ignoring the prompt because you can.

MF: A lot of them are newly exited. And that's why I want to get your views on things in terms of forming the "right" way to exit. Hearing about other exited entrepreneurs' experiences has forced me to think more about the importance of clarity and *ikigai*. I want to know in more detail how you charted your path in a certain direction with your exit.

What went on in your head? What steps did you take to prepare yourself? What do you wish you did differently if anything?

JJ: So three months after I exited my company, everything came to a head and I ended up getting divorced within a year of the exit. It was fine, though. She got half of the proceeds of the company, but, you know, still a shitload of money. She was there with me for a long time. Some relationships do end up working out. But certainly, the common thing with entrepreneurs is that you are always in growth mode, both business and professional, and if your spouse is not on that same plane, then the gap between you will keep getting bigger and bigger and bigger. Because you're just growing and growing and all of that is compounding, while the other person remains the same.

One of the things I wish I had done—and maybe she wouldn't have been interested in this—but I wish I had talked to her more about the business, to have been more open about the challenges I was facing at the time.

The other thing is, there were events that I went to by myself where I probably should have had her join me. Manufacturing is pretty freaking boring, but some of the trade shows and some of the conferences—that may have allowed her to awaken that spirit within herself. Maybe it's there, maybe it's not, so that's one thing to consider while on the journey. She didn't want to be involved in the company at all and I respected that. But she should have—rather, *I* should have—been more vocal with her about things.

Another consideration is that you might exit for life-changing money and you have that paradox of too much optionality.

That was one of the things that prompted me to take certain directives: It's Derek Sivers', "Hell yes" mentality [Sivers is the author of the book *Hell Yeah or No: What's Worth Doing*]. I use that phrase now and think about it a lot, which is to say, "Thank you, and no." So saying "no" and creating space for opportunities to open up what you want to do, which is hard because you're used to having all your time to yourself.

Maybe, as you're an entrepreneur going along, you go beyond the golf and the surfing and think about what you really want to do. One of the things Dan Sullivan [founder of Strategic Coach] will say is to "Look back to when you were six or seven years old. What did you do for fun?" I used to run around the woods. I still like running around in the woods. So that helps you narrow down some of the many options vying for your time.

I've always wanted to learn how to play a musical instrument. I didn't just go out and buy a little keyboard, I bought a Baby Grand and I have a good space to put it in my living room. Because of that expense, it's more likely that I'm gonna say, "I can't waste that money so I know I'll use it." It's about having that list of what you want to do ready so when you do exit you're not trying to make it all up suddenly. Being prepared makes it less likely that you will be influenced by whatever is en vogue for the day, or your friends or whatever. I'm thinking, you know, I'm still figuring it out, like a lot of entrepreneurs. Although I've never been diagnosed, I probably have ADD, so

I'm just always going after shiny objects when it's hard being able to focus. It's sort of weird, being able to say you could take a year and just do anything because it's only a year, right? So one of the things is, I've tried to get serious about sprinting as a sport and I'm prioritizing that as much as possible so I can compete in the nationals next July. My goal is to make the finals for my age group.

MF: You're the 400 meters, right?

JJ: Yeah, the 400 meters. I qualified for the 200, so I will probably run that, too. But I don't think I have the natural speed to be in the finals, and I don't know if I'll get in the finals, but it's something I want to do. Getting out of your rut, just doing different things.

Last October, I spent the month in Argentina, mostly in Buenos Aires. I had always brushed the desire away, telling myself that being away for a month would be too long. But it was a really cool experience. I went to Peru to the deep, deep jungle. And you've heard Paul Rosolie [an American conservationist and author of the memoir *Mother of God*] on any of the podcasts, but he went down there, too. He and his partners built a 110-foot-high tree house in the jungle and I stayed there with them. That was insane, waking up to the howler monkeys and the birds, being right in the heart of things. What an experience! This is like a hardcore way out in the jungle. You really can't go any further. It wasn't even a lodge. So taking those chances that are not really "chances," but just disappearing into nature is so wonderful. I'm trying to structure my life so that if I want to disappear for three months and have no phone contact or email or whatever, I can do it. I got involved with way too many things after I sold my company that I'm not into anymore today, so I'm still trying to untangle some of those things.

MF: I remember when you exited initially and you were looking to build a fitness center.

JJ: That was quasi-successful. The lesson learned is that there are a lot of people who do real estate and that it is not a more competency-based, unique talent. The other lesson is, I lease space to some business owners and those are, more or less, okay. But then I couldn't get anybody to do the recovery center, so I sort of created one myself. I couldn't get anybody to do the yoga or pilates bar, right? I learned I'm not a detailed operational person, though I recognize how necessary it is to line the right people up to take care of things like hiring. So right now I'm trying to sell the facility. I would keep my office there and I'd have my sprint track there. That was helpful at the time because when I bought the building, Phoenix wasn't on the horizon and there's not as much need now to have a sprint track in New Hampshire in the winter, but the facility is still there. The biggest thing is that I locked up a lot of capital in an asset that's not producing a return, so I'd rather deploy that capital to other places.

MF: And you mentioned a company that you've funded and a team you've invested in. Can you tell me more about that?

JJ: That's something that I've gotten a lot of clarity on recently. I've been thinking about the phrase that's come up for me: having high agency. I realized my co-founder has a lot of high agency. He's the epitome of that. Then I thought about my team. I had three direct reports when I sold my company: my assistant, my president and then my marketing manager, who has incredibly high agency. *He* managed *me*. He was the type of guy who just threw all these little odd projects at me. What that made me realize is that I love starting companies. Paperless Parts started out providing seed capital and supplying domain expertise in manufacturing as well as in the general business. And then I was a coach, mentor, confidant and advisor to this person to the point that he's outgrown me.

The company is valued more than what I sold my company for. I work—I'm Chairman of the Cap Board—but I work a few hours a week and I'm the largest shareholder. So obviously, a huge win technically, and I have fun with it. It never seemed like a chore, except for the board meetings. I hate those. What I've decided is that I want to create companies so other people can run them. My co-founder was 30 years old when I started, 38 now and it is life-changing for him. My eyes are open and I am looking for high-agency, 30-something individuals for whom starting a company would be life-changing—it would give them, essentially, freedom of money, and that's how I figured out how I want to proceed with businesses in the future: by starting companies. So probably not for everybody, but at least for me, that's an "Aha!" moment. I am trying to put myself on the path of those types of high-agency people.

I've got a ton of ideas, I just need the right people. So in [Strategic] Coach parlance, there are people who "make it up," people who "make it real" and people who "make it recur." I make it up. And my partner, Jason, and my former Marketing Manager, Matt—they're both incredible—they are very "make it real" people, especially as a team. So it's not so much that I need a business but that I need "make it real" people who can work within the framework of ideas I give them.

MF: I like where your mind is—having a good message of what can happen after you sell a company. I've talked to a few exited entrepreneurs where the whole process of selling their company is a huge added stress. Additional stressors might come from divorce, or with some debilitating type of illness that occurs at the same time as the exit.

JJ: One of the things I did was use the Strategic Coach tool, the "Impact Filter." So in my case, I decided ahead of my exit what had to be true the day after the sale for me. There were 11 things I submitted, and I got 10 out of the 11. I caved a little bit on the number, but one of the 11 was that I had to have unfettered access to be involved in Paperless Parts. They said, "No, you can be an investor, but that is it." And, you know, this was a nine-figure deal.

I called up the CEO one day and I just said, "You know what, if I can't do this my way, then I don't want to sell the company."

And she said, "Well, you can't do that."

I said, "Okay, well, then I guess we're done." And I felt so good about it. That was on a Tuesday and on that Friday, I got a call and they capitulated. It wasn't a bluff when I drew that line in the sand. It's just one of the things that I knew I needed to do to be happy. I would encourage all entrepreneurs to do that.

MF: Amazing advice. That is a game-changer, right there.

JJ: Yeah and I kept it written and folded up in my wallet so I would remember to look at it. The other thing I would do is I would probably hire some retired lawyer to manage the other fucking lawyers (my lawyers, not the other side's) because they end up running up costly fees. It was my first deal and I knew jack shit, and I didn't push back enough. The bottom line is, I didn't know where to push back exactly. I could have pushed for more. It's not the cost that is the factor, but the stress, the reduction of stress. And so that's a great job for retired transaction lawyers who don't want a full-time job, but still want to be in the game a little bit, to make a little money.

MF: Well, it eases your stress, too. I mean, imagine that.

JJ: Absolutely. So we owned the building, and we leased it back to the buyer. The lawyers probably got $10000 in fees because they came back with this one-sided lease instead of coming back with something fair, and I was like, fuckin' A, I should have pushed back and I should have just said, "No, I'm not paying for the fees that you created for this. Give me something fair and I'll charge before what you just did." Bullshit. And that's a small example. You've probably seen a lot of this stuff, too.

MF: I have. I love the idea of just looking back, having that list, the Impact Filter list. That is key. It sounds like you had a realistic expectation of the fact that you weren't just going to sit around, literally and figuratively. I believe staying active is a core part of who you are.

JJ: Things have changed in terms of my bottom line now that I've done a lot of the work on myself. That sort of started in 2021 when I did some somatic release and then the Ayahuasca and then another plant-based medicine that is relatively unknown. I've got some other stuff that I wish I'd done earlier because that would have probably given me more peace and more clarity.

MF: Probably pre-sale, right?

JJ: Oh, yeah. The other thing is that your executive team gets pulled into all that once you've decided to exit. But that means you are not executing. So basically, the buyer shoots you down on price, because you're not hitting your mark. Then I learned to be like, "Here are our projections for 2025, however, since we are involved in the sale with you, then obviously my executive team is going to be spending 50 percent of the time on that transaction. So we're going to cut these numbers down by 50 percent to reflect the lack of attention on the business due to the transaction. And you have our history to know that once the transactions are out of the way, we'll execute again. But we are not going to have you complain about poor numbers this year and put that stake in the ground. These are the expectations." I would even have had people sign off on it. They would hate to do that, but that's when you get to somebody who's buying a business for what it is, as opposed to just viewing it as a financial transaction.

Then there are these little things. Even though my last day was the day of the sale, I would insist people just find fucking health insurance first. I need to be an employee for three years, or whatever it takes to be on the health insurance plan. You know, pay me $10000 a year, whatever the minimum is for me to be a full-time employee, get insurance and I want a car allowance, too. Think carefully about those things that you have as expenses and maybe they give you a lump sum of $50000 a year for the next three years, right? They may say, "We'll just fucking add it to the sale." Then you have to have the discipline, maybe, to allocate $50000 into an account or whatever and say, "Okay, this is for the use of all those incidentals." Yeah, it's all these mind games you play there.

MF: What's your next move? Do you plan to spend time in any place in particular, given that business has you kind of spread out in different states?

JJ: My goal is to spend time with family in Boston. I'm just letting myself be open. And this is one of the things, really, for clarity with the synchronicities I've been experiencing.

When I was in Peru, my buddy and I wanted to do things that the locals would do, not just be the tourists and drop in. We met this woman in Lima who had a car. She drove us to a city where we ended up down on the beach at sunset in this bar, overlooking the water and watching the surface and it was just like being in Malibu. I met a woman I really liked and had fun with her. Bottom line, she has two kids going to college in the US. She was already coming over here at the end of June, so I connected with her in Washington state. She ended up spending the summer with me and she'll be coming back in two months. She has a 10-year visa and I'll be going down to Peru in a little bit, which I haven't planned out fully yet.

I am just going with the flow. I guess that's another thing: I've put myself out into the world to open myself up to the synchronicities that happen when I'm in alignment. I'm more aware of them and attuned to their subtleties. I call them synchronicities and then I trust that they're there for me. The universe has my best interest in mind, which I believe fully now more than ever.

AFTERWORD

I can't profess to know what it's like to read the insights of the brilliant and authentic entrepreneurs featured in this book, but I know that speaking to them about the topics encompassed here transformed me.

My hope is that no matter where you are in the process—someone who's exited a business or someone who hopes to do so one day—you've gained a clearer picture of all the possibilities in front of you.

In these pages, some of the greatest minds of our time have shared their experiences of navigating the turbulent waters of enterprise from startup to post-exit life, where they've grappled with mental health challenges ranging from anxiety and depression to burnout and existential angst ultimately leading to life-changing transformation. These fundamental changes cause huge metamorphoses in most cases.

It is a gift to watch others find a higher calling unveiled to them once darkness, chaos and confusion slowly disappear from their lives. Their stories aren't just narratives of struggle, but demonstrations of resilience, reinvention and profound shifts. From navigating the emotional rollercoaster of transition to redefining success on their own terms, each story is a beacon of hope for anyone seeking solace and support in the next chapter of their journey.

By facing these issues head-on through the brave and brilliant stories of our contributors, we are actively removing the subject of mental health out of the shadows, shedding the taboo, saving lives and changing the face of the future for so many people who encounter challenges with their mental health.

That's why this book is not just for entrepreneurs, though we are a unique group; it is for anyone who has ever faced a moment of reckoning or struggled to find purpose and meaning in their lives. These stories serve as a reminder that success is not measured by external accolades, but by the richness of our inner lives, the depth of our relationships and the resilience of our spirits. May we all find our higher purpose, climb our second mountain and embody the *ikigai* within ourselves.

ACKNOWLEDGMENTS

This book would not be possible without the willingness and courage of countless entrepreneurs and practitioners who shared their experiences with me in the most courageous and self-effacing ways. I am forever indebted to my best friend, Blake, whose extraordinary journey inspires me to continue to help others find their higher purpose. I am grateful that he reminds me that support systems are available to anyone–and especially to exited entrepreneurs—that can improve mental health while also building a strong community. I have the utmost respect and admiration for anyone taking the chance to exit their companies, leaning into the unknown reality that awaits.

I want to thank my parents, Kiyomi and Dot, for their love and for instilling in me the beautiful wisdom of both our Japanese and Chinese cultures. A very heartfelt thank you belongs to the team at Legacy Launch Pad Publishing, for representing and advocating for this work. To my editors, Anna David, Ryan Aliapoulios and Lucy Hartman: thank you for approaching this project with excitement, vision and diligence. I am eternally grateful to my late mentor, Larry, the very embodiment of *ikigai*, who lived his higher purpose by showing me and others how to live ours.

I am the luckiest guy in the world to have the family, friends, business associates and now readers that I do. Thank you.

ABOUT THE AUTHOR

Mark Fujiwara has worked as a Certified Portfolio Manager for nearly three decades. As a Director at Baird, he approaches wealth management holistically, not only helping individuals build legacies that encompass high character, but also expanding capital by aligning with personal values. Mark continues to align his values with a higher purpose as a Certified Exit Planning Advisor and the CFO and board member of A Reading World, a non-profit that provides books and libraries for students and children in developing countries in Africa. Mark earned a Bachelor of Science degree in Business Administration and Finance at the University of California, Riverside and continued his education at Columbia Business School.

Mark fuses his vast knowledge of investment and financial planning with experiential knowledge of mental health and recovery. He lives and works within the spiritual concept of *ikigai*–the Japanese practice of doing what you love with the gifts you have, in order to provide for your family with both financial and emotional capital. Mark recently embarked on the highly specialized journey of the exit entrepreneur, having gathered hard-won wisdom along the way to help other exiting, growing and newly-minted entrepreneurs discover their higher purpose.

Though Mark does not consider himself an "exited"

entrepreneur (yet), he continues his work in wealth management while creating opportunities for other high-net-worth entrepreneurs to form inclusive communities built on the shared values of trust, integrity, empathy and service.

Mark lives with his wife, Amy and their daughter, Stella in Marin County, California. He spends his days elevating others, hiking trails, running marathons, doing the occasional cold plunge and practicing Japanese calligraphy—all things in service to the *flow*.

For more information about Mark Fujiwara,
scan the QR code below:

ABOUT THE PUBLISHER

Legacy Launch Pad is a boutique publishing company that works with entrepreneurs from all over the world.

For more information about Legacy Launch Pad Publishing, go to: www.legacylaunchpadpub.com.